European
Cycling

European Cycling

THE 20 CLASSIC RACES

by Noel Henderson

VITESSE PRESS
BRATTLEBORO, VERMONT

Maps copyright © 1988 by Carpress International, except map on page 108 © 1989 by FPL
Corporation.

Photos copyright © 1989 by: Ed Oudenaarden: page 48; Sergio Penazzo: pages 9, 60, 62, 132
(right), back cover, upper and lower left; Presse Sports: pages xxi, 32, 52, 70, 83, 90, 96, 98, 106,
110, 111, 115, 121, 132 (left); Presse Sports / Col. Laget: page 68; H. A. Roth: pages 84, 94; Cor
Vos: pages 4, 10, 15, 20, 26, 33, 34, 38, 41, 44, 55, 74, 78, 80, 86, 116, back cover, upper and
lower right.

ISBN 0-941950-20-4
Library of Congress catalog card number 89-51233

Cover and text design by Irving Perkins Associates

Published by Vitesse Press
A division of FPL Corporation
Brattleboro, VT 05302

Second printing February 1990

Manufactured in the United States of America

to René Jacobs

One of the important qualities of enthusiasm is the desire to communicate it.

—Bernard Levin

Contents

ABOUT THE AUTHOR

Noel Henderson is deputy headmaster of a secondary school in northern England, where his main teaching subject is English. His interest in cycling began when he started touring in the mid 1950s, about the time when Louison Bobet made history by becoming the first rider to win the Tour de France in three successive years.

Although Henderson remained a dedicated tourist, his interest in racing grew, particularly when he lived in France for 18 months. This was when the great British rider Tom Simpson, whom Henderson knew, was beginning to make a name for himself on the Continent.

On returning to England, Henderson became active in the administration of British cycling. He led more than 20 school cycling club tours to the various corners of Britain and mainland Europe. He also co-founded the English Schools' Cycling Association.

Henderson is the author of four other books on cycling. The first, *Continental Cycle Racing*, was published in 1970, and was a precursor to *European Cycling*. He has also been an active cycling journalist, writing for *International Cycle Sport*, *Pro News* (which he also edited), and, more recently, *Cycling Weekly*.

Henderson is married, with three grown children. In his spare time, when not teaching or writing about cycling, Henderson is a senior trade union official.

Preface

When I wrote *Continental Cycle Racing* almost 20 years ago there were very few books in English about professional cycling. None covered the major European races systematically, although one or two touched upon them incidentally. Since then there has been a dramatic increase in information about cycling.

Now books on training, coaching, and diet are readily available, as are race stories, biographies, and yearbooks. Cycling magazines give vivid details of the world's top races, often supported by fine color photography. Television has also made an impact—the coverage may be sporadic and the editing may leave something to be desired, but it is at least possible to see the Tour de France, the world championship, or Paris-Roubaix. And there is a small but growing library of videocassette tapes of the more well-known races.

I don't know if I wanted to write another book about the top races and riders because of these developments or in spite of them. I do write from a different point of view now. My first book was that of an enthusiastic archivist who hoped to fill a gap in cycling literature. During the past decades I have seen many of the famous races, spoken to many of the top riders, visited the Continent regularly, and written for two cycling magazines. I still want to write about it all.

Some years ago I was asked to cover the British national road championship, held around 17 laps of an urban circuit. The organizer had thoughtfully provided a minibus and driver for the press. On the first lap, two of my colleagues seemed more interested in the pubs en route than the race. On the second lap they asked to be deposited at the hostelry of their choice, to be collected on the last lap.

I hope that familiarity never breeds such contempt in my case. Perhaps I am fortunate to have a full-time job outside cycling. I am certainly lucky in being able to call upon the advice of some of Europe's top cycling journalists. To René Jacobs in particular I wish to offer my warmest thanks.

Monsieur Jacobs was formerly editor-in-chief of *Vélo*, the cycling annual that is the standard reference for writers. For 15 years he has been answering most of my questions. When he had no answer, he could always refer me to some one who did.

I have a confession to make.

None of the great writers on cycling was around when Maurice Garin or Octave Lapize was riding. Very few were born when Eugène Christophe smashed his forks during a Pyrenean stage of the Tour de France, rode or ran to the nearest blacksmith's shop, lit the forge, and carried out his own repairs.

But this story and others like it are the essential legends of cycling. There are many in this book. I didn't witness Christophe's plight, nor do I necessarily have firsthand knowledge of all the tales herein. I don't even know where I first read or heard the story, since it is recounted in so many books published in France and Belgium.

There is no copyright on fact, but some writers may consider presentations of fact or interpretations of races their own. Where the legends of cycling are concerned, there appears to be a great freemasonry. Not only is it expected that anybody writing about the Tour, for example, will recount Christophe's tragedy, it is understood that there is no sense of plagiarism in such matters.

So I offer my thanks to the many writers on cycling whose books I have read over the last 30 years. It would be impossible for me to name them individually, for I have built my own collection of cycling legends from many sources.

If, one day, some writer uses this book as a source, I hope that I shall have the wisdom, and the enthusiasm, to feel both pleased and flattered.

ABBREVIATIONS
OF RIDERS' NATIONALITIES

A	Australia	I	Italy
Au	Austria	Ir	Ireland
B	Belgium	N	Norway
Ca	Canada	Nl	Netherlands
Co	Colombia	P	Portugal
D	Denmark	Sd	Sweden
F	France	Sp	Spain
L	Luxembourg	Sw	Switzerland
G	Germany (pre-World War II)	US	United States
GB	Great Britain	WG	West Germany

Introduction

Imagine a sport that's fast, dangerous, and colorful, a grueling sport whose athletes train fulltime, year-round and compete as many as seven hours daily for up to 20 successive days, rain or shine (and sometimes snow).

Imagine a professional sport in which team sponsorship can cost $5 million a year and top athletes make as much as $500,000 and yet the events are free to the spectators—there's no stadium and no admission charge.

Imagine a vehicular sport where man is the motor, a sport that combines the flash of fine-tuned, high-tech machinery with the down-to-earth drama of men and muscles.

That's bicycle road racing.

Bicycle racing is one of the world's most popular sports, and nowhere more so than in Europe. It's estimated that 20 million spectators line the course during the three-week Tour de France every July. There are many kinds of bicycle races. Some take place on public roads and others on specially constructed tracks called velodromes. There are currently 11 cycling events in the Olympics, ranging in length from a minute to five hours. The annual world championship has more than 20 events, for men and women, amateurs and professionals.

One-day, point-to-point races dominate the professional road racing calendar in Europe. The most prestigious of these are known as classics. Stage races are the other common form of competition for the top riders. These events are a series of point-to-point races and often include time trials. Stage races last for several days—or weeks—and travel over meandering routes that offer a variety of topographic conditions and challenges. There are several well-known stage races. Most famous is the Tour de France, known simply as the Tour.

Which are the top 20 races and how have they been chosen? Some go back almost a century, others little more than 20 years. In *Continental*

Cycle Racing (Pelham Books, 1970), I described the "fourteen races which attract the best and largest fields, and victory in which brings the greatest prestige and most lucrative contracts." The influence of the defunct Super Prestige Pernod competition on my choices is significant. The Pernod was virtually a world championship on points. Promoters knew that the inclusion of their race in the competition would almost guarantee success, but they also knew that the rules were strict. When the course of the Flèche Wallonne was changed one year so that it became a stroll instead of a struggle, the race was penalized by being allocated half as many Pernod points the following year. The organizer was warned that unless the hilly formula was readopted the race would be dropped from the series.

Some races have no such problems. Who can doubt that the Tour is the target for all aspiring stars, or that every rider dreams of being world champion? At least 80% of the several hundred licensed professionals who rode in 1988 would have been happy with a single victory—Paris-Roubaix. These three are the top races in the world.

Through the successes of Charly Gaul, Jacques Anquetil and Eddy Merckx, the Tour of Italy (Giro) developed from a peninsular parade into an international race, arguably as important as Paris-Roubaix. Next most significant are three classics, all of considerable physical difficulty. Liège-Bastogne-Liège is held in the Belgian Ardennes region and is hilly on the outward journey and far worse on the return. The Tour of Flanders has few hills for its first hundred miles—just the numbing wind of the Flanders plain—but then takes cobbled climbs of 20% grades, ensuring that only the tough finish at the front. The Tour of Lombardy climbs higher than either of the other two, twisting over the passes surrounding Lake Como, before the route plunges into the town of Como from the final summit.

Next in importance are three classics and a stage race. The Flèche Wallonne is only marginally less difficult than Liège-Bastogne-Liège, but it owes its lower classification to the fact that it is a midweek race, where the quality of the field is liable to be reduced. Milan-San Remo is Italy's number two classic, less severe than the Tour of Lombardy, but with a magnificent course and often an exciting finish caused by the Poggio climb and the descent to the outskirts of San Remo itself. Paris-Tours, with its relatively flat course, has often been a contest among sprinters. But it has also frequently been won by a lone breakaway in the closing miles, with the sprinters left to battle for second place. The Tour of Spain (Vuelta) has a checkered history, having become an important international race only in the mid 1950s. It also suffers from scheduling conflicts with as many as five classics, usually leading to an impoverished field.

Three classics follow in my ranking, and many will claim that I have downgraded them unfairly. Bordeaux-Paris, oldest of all, is often known as the Derby, although the name is misleading since it is a race for the stayer rather than the sprinter. Since World War II it has failed to occupy a fixed place on the international calendar and has sometimes been cancelled. Amateurs have been included in recent years in an attempt to overcome the recurring problem of a very small field. The Grand Prix of Nations also has a small field and has also moved around a great deal, but its present base in Cannes is the most suitable yet. These two are the unconventional classics, the former being a paced race for part of its distance and the latter a time trial. Third in this group is Paris-Brussels, which was once a rival to Paris-Roubaix. Since World War II, traffic problems have caused its cancellation in several years and a change to a midweek date has done little for its reputation.

Those 14 were described in my first book. Now, 20 years later, another six deserve inclusion. The Amstel Gold Race, though the newest, has acquired a considerable reputation in a relatively short time. Contrary to expectations, it is less flat than its Dutch setting might suggest. Ghent-Wevelgem, though short on natural difficulties and sometimes regarded as a training race for Paris-Roubaix, is a fine event in its own right. The Tour of Henniger Tower, held in the Taunus Mountains outside Frankfurt, is one of Europe's great cycling spectacles. Traditionally held on May 1, it usually clashes with the Vuelta, but often attracts a fine international field. It used to be followed a day or two later by the Zürich Championship, a race held on a long circuit, but the Swiss race was moved to mid August in 1988. Het Volk has no scheduling problems, just the weather to contend with. The earliest of the top 20 on the calendar, it is the first major test of early season fitness.

Finally there is the Tour of Switzerland, easily the most demanding of the shorter stage races. Though it is sometimes entered as training for the Tour, its double crossing of the Alps earns it a reputation of its own and it has been won by a number of notable riders, especially in recent years.

These are my top 20. Several of these races go back almost a century, others little more than 20 years. Nearly all were regularly included in the defunct Super Prestige Pernod competition, and that significantly influenced my choices. Some will disagree with the selection; many will disagree with the points which I have assigned to each (see appendix), but one must stop somewhere. I hope that my selection of 15 one-day classics, four national stage races, and the world championship has a justification of its own.

If this book has a theme, it's the growing internationalization of bicycle racing, and what that has meant for the sport. Since the start of international competition in the mid 19th century, riders from three countries—Belgium, France, and Italy—have dominated the classics and stage races. But there have been significant differences between riders of different nationalities. The Belgians have been the kings of the classics, while the Italians and French have proven better at winning stage races. More important than these distinctions, however, is the increasing success, since the end of World War II, of riders from other countries.

This trend is clearly illustrated in the Giro, the national tour of Italy. From 1909 to 1949 the top three places were always filled by Italians, except for one third and two second places taken by Belgians Marcel Buysse and Joseph Demuysère. In 1950 Hugo Koblet of Switzerland became the first foreign winner when he beat Gino Bartali by 5:12. Since 1950, Italians have filled all top three places on only six occasions. Foreigners have won 17 of 39 Giros, and three times—in 1972, 1987 and 1988—have filled the top three spots.

The first reason for increasing success by riders from countries other than Belgium, France, and Italy is the proliferation of races. When Maurice Garin won the first Tour de France in 1903, only two of the other top 20 races described in this book existed. By 1909, the number had risen to eight. A decade later, Henri Pélissier could compete in 11 of the current top 20. In 1932, Alfredo Binda could compete in 13 and after the second world war, Fausto Coppi had 17 from which to choose.

International bicycle racing started in France in 1869 when James Moore won Paris-Rouen. For the next 40 years or so France hosted all the top races, although Liège-Bastogne-Liège (Belgium) was promoted three times—the earliest in 1894—before becoming firmly established in 1930. In 1905 came the Tour of Lombardy (Italy), followed over the years by a host of others including the Zürich Championship (Switzerland), the world championship (roving), and in 1936 the Tour of Spain. The newest of the 20 most important races are the Henniger Tower Grand Prix (West Germany), begun in 1962, and the Amstel Gold Race, started in the Netherlands in 1966. As racing spread to different countries, riders other than the Belgians, the Italians, and the French had more opportunity for serious competition. The improvement of international transportation was the second change that led to increased international competition. Starting with the German autobahn program between the world wars, expanding with the reconstruction of railways from 1945, and continuing into the current age of intercontinental air travel, the increasing ease of getting from one place to another has revolutionized bicycle racing. Nowadays, riders think little of driving 400 miles between races on successive days. In 1965, Jacques Anquetil hired a plane to take him from the finish of the

Cycling fans hoping for a good view and sponsors seeking the best exposure for their logos compete for space near the finish line. Here, Roger de Vlaeminck, left, takes the 1971 Flèche Wallonne from Frans Verbeeck.

Dauphiné Libéré stage race (which he had won) to the start of Bordeaux-Paris (which he also won). And it will not be many more years before the Tour visits the North American continent.

Sponsorship from outside the sport is the third development that has led to increasing participation—and success—of riders from other nations. Fiorenzi Magni won the Italian championship, the Tour of Flanders, and the Giro in 1951. Nevertheless, at the start of the next season he was worried about his ability to afford his racing, and turned to the Nivea company, a cosmetics manufacturer, in his quest for support. The result was the introduction of rider and team sponsorship by companies which were not directly involved in bicycling, just when television producers were starting to take an interest in the sport. When the members of the Fagor team offer themselves for sale collectively for about half a billion dollars, the importance of such sponsorship becomes clear. Equally clear is that no company is likely to spend a fortune on a pro cycling team unless it can be quite sure of getting a good return on its investment.

The growing number of races across Europe, improvements to public transportation, and the introduction of outside sponsorship have led to the internationalization of cycling. Many individuals have contributed to this process, but three riders stand out.

First was Brian Robinson, a member of the British team entered in the 1955 Tour by Hercules Cycles. Robinson performed well. He stuck with

Continental racing and was the first Briton to become an established member of the peloton. Then came American Audrey McElmury, whose victory in the women's road race at the 1969 worlds justified the transatlantic investment in cycling. Finally, there was a Colombian, Alfonso Flores, who won the 1980 Tour de l'Avenir by brilliantly aggressive riding at a time when the Soviets and East Germans were dominating amateur racing. He was followed by two whole teams from Colombia, just as Robinson was followed by Tom Simpson, Barry Hoban, and Robert Millar, and McElmury by Jonathan Boyer and Greg LeMond.

Other nations have followed: Phil Anderson has come from Australia, Steve Bauer from Canada, Raul Alcala from Mexico, and Sean Kelly and Stephen Roche have followed the path from Ireland first trodden by Seamus Elliott in the mid 1950s.

Scandinavia is also producing excellent professional cyclists, with Dag-Otto Lauritzen and Kim Andersen to the fore. Great Britain has Robert Millar now, Malcolm Elliott and Joey McLoughlin for the future.

It is interesting to note that the International Professional Cycling Federation (FICP) standings, which are based on performances over the three most recent years, included no Belgians, one Italian and two Frenchmen in the top ten at the end of 1988.

New races are becoming established races on the international calendar, such as the Clasico R.C.N. in Colombia, the Nissan International in Ireland, and the Coors Classic in the states, although the latter may be without a sponsor for 1989. Even races in Australia are beginning to attract the attention of European riders who don't want to spend the winter riding cyclocross.

The internationalization of cycling continues.

Predictions are dangerous. The late David Saunders, probably the most influential cycling journalist writing for a British newspaper, claimed in *Cycling in the Sixties* (Pelham Books, 1971) that the 1970s would see British riders win the Tour and the Grand Prix of Nations, and that Britain would promote a classic that would be covered on European television. None of those things has yet happened. Nevertheless, it seems reasonably safe to predict that by the end of the century riders from the United States, Britain, Australia, Ireland, the Netherlands, Spain, and Colombia will have joined the new heroes from Belgium, Italy, and France as regular winners of the most prestigious races.

European
Cycling

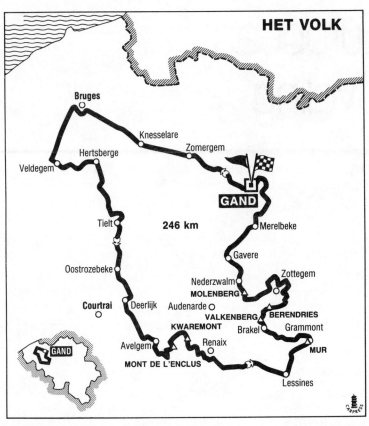

HET VOLK

246 km

GAND

1945	Bogaerts (B)	1960	not held	1975	Bruyère (B)
1946	Pieters (B)	1961	de Cabooter (B)	1976	Peeters, W. (B)
1947	Sercu (B)	1962	de Middeleir (B)	1977	Maertens (B)
1948	Grysolle (B)	1963	van Meenen (B)	1978	Maertens (B)
1949	de Clerck (B)	1964	Melckenbeeck (B)	1979	de Vlaeminck (B)
1950	de Clerck (B)	1965	de Pauw (B)	1980	Bruyère (B)
1951	Bogaerts (B)	1966	de Roo (Nl)	1981	Raas (Nl)
1952	Sterckx (B)	1967	Vekemans (B)	1982	de Wolf, A. (B)
1953	Sterckx (B)	1968	van Springel (B)	1983	de Wolf, A. (B)
1954	de Baere (B)	1969	de Vlaeminck (B)	1984	Planckaert, E. (B)
1955	Anthonis (B)	1970	Verbeeck (B)	1985	Planckaert, E. (B)
1956	Sterckx (B)	1971	Merckx (B)	1986	cancelled
1957	Kherkove (B)	1972	Verbeeck (B)	1987	van Vliet, T. (Nl)
1958	Planckaert, J. (B)	1973	Merckx (B)	1988	van Holen (B)
1959	Elliott (Ir)	1974	Bruyère (B)		

SPEED RECORD: Joseph Bruyère, 43.352 kph in 1975
MOST VICTORIES: Joseph Bruyère, and Ernest Sterckx, 3 each

Het Volk

Het Volk is the name of both a Belgian newspaper and a Belgian race. It's no coincidence that the names are the same since the race was born of the competition for readers and prestige between two Flemish newspapers. One of those newspapers had created the Tour of Flanders in 1913 and later, another event held near Brussels. Immediately after World War II the directors of the Ghent daily, *Het Volk*, created a rival race—Het Volk—to boost the circulation of their own newspaper.

Since it takes place on the last Saturday in February (occasionally the first Saturday in March) Het Volk is the first major test of the season, particularly for Belgian riders. Its date makes Het Volk susceptible to the weather. In 1986 four inches of snow fell the night before the race, forcing it to be cancelled.

The rigors of the Flemish climate in late winter may explain the lack of success in Het Volk by foreign riders. After weeks of training and pre-season racing in the warm Mediterranean sunshine, few southern European riders are prepared for North Sea gales, frozen cobblestones, or the army of Flemish riders and their supporters, avid for a home victory.

Although no foreigner won Het Volk until its 15th year, it almost happened in 1948 when Fausto Coppi was first over the line. In those days it was illegal for a rider with a mechanical problem to receive help from a teammate. Coppi had punctured and was given a wheel illicitly. He chased, caught the peloton, and went on to win, but the rules relegated him to second behind Sylvain Grysolle. In 1959 Irishman Seamus Elliott managed to overcome the local coalitions with a surprise win at record speed, but generally the Flemish have made the race their own.

One exception to the Flemish domination was Joseph Bruyère, for many years the faithful lieutenant of Eddy Merckx, but a fine rider in his own right with five classic victories. Bruyère's Het Volk story began in 1974. Despite a heavy snowfall the previous day, the race was contested under a blue sky. With 50 miles to go the field was thinned to half, with Merckx's

Garbed in gloves, booties, and rain gear, Jan Raas leads the pack up the slick Kwaremont in Het Volk. Unfavorable weather and cobbled climbs typify the spring classics.

Molteni team in charge. Up the notorious Mur de Grammont Merckx escaped with Frans Verbeeck, the latter in no way incapacitated by having left his false teeth behind on the Côte d'Azur. But this was only a practice raid. After they were caught, a Molteni rider attacked on every hill, with the Flemish watching keenly and sitting on Merckx. Finally the inevitable happened—one man was allowed a little too much freedom. It was Bruyère, and he got away alone up the Grotenberg. He increased his lead steadily and was two minutes clear with six miles to go when tragedy intervened.

The driver of a car failed to notice Bruyère changing position on the road. The car clipped Bruyère's rear wheel, throwing him onto the pavement and smashing his bike. Despite multiple contusions to his left elbow and although unable to bend his left knee, Bruyère seized a spare bike and managed to continue alone to the finish and win. There, a crowd applauded his courage, forgetting for the moment that he wasn't Flemish or even a native Belgian, having been born in Maastricht, just across the Dutch border.

The next year saw attack after attack, little of it serious, for Het Volk is a *course des primes*, where a rider who stays away for 20 miles or so can pick up more cash than the race winner. By the last climb, the Volkegemberg, the favorites were at the front. Frans Verbeeck got away with Bruyère on his wheel. With Merckx blocking, Roger de Vlaeminck joined them. As Verbeeck and de Vlaeminck watched each other and the chasers closed, Bruyère slipped away alone to win again, this year free from trouble and not needing three months to recuperate.

It was not until 1980 that Bruyère completed his hat trick, and then it was a surprise. Merckx had retired and Bruyère, overweight and suffering from conjunctivitis, was riding for the Flandria team. For 100 miles Kim Andersen and Wilfried Wesemael were away, 10 minutes clear at one time. They were caught by de Vlaeminck and a small bunch at the foot of the last climb, where Gerrie Knetemann escaped. The race looked over but Marc de Meyer led the chase and again everyone was together.

When Bruyère took a flier nobody bothered to chase, confident that he would find the remaining seven miles too much, given his lack of form. With one lap of the finishing circuit to go he was 12 seconds clear and had just over a mile to ride to the second and final crossing of the line. First into the last corner, he had time to slip his chain onto a specially fitted 12-tooth sprocket. At the line his lead was only six seconds, but it was enough for Bruyère to establish himself as the hero of Het Volk.

1907	Petit-Breton (F)				
1908	van Hauwaert (B)				
1909	Ganna (I)				
1910	Christophe (F)				
1911	Garrigou (F)				
1912	Pélissier, H. (F)				
1913	Defraye (B)				
1914	Agostoni (I)				
1915	Corlaita (I)				
1916	not held				
1917	Belloni (I)				
1918	Girardengo (I)				
1919	Gremo (I)				
1920	Belloni (I)				
1921	Girardengo (I)				
1922	Brunero (I)				
1923	Girardengo (I)				
1924	Linari (I)				
1925	Girardengo (I)				
1926	Girardengo (I)				
1927	Chesi (I)				
1928	Girardengo (I)				
1929	Binda (I)				
1930	Mara (I)				
1931	Binda (I)				
1932	Bovet (I)				
1933	Guerra (I)				

MILAN–SAN REMO 1988

1934	Demuysère (B)	1953	Petrucci (I)	1971	Merckx (B)
1935	Olmo (I)	1954	van Steenbergen (B)	1972	Merckx (B)
1936	Varetto (I)	1955	Derycke (B)	1973	de Vlaeminck (B)
1937	del Cancia (I)	1956	de Bruyne (B)	1974	Gimondi (I)
1938	Olmo (I)	1957	Poblet (Sp)	1975	Merckx (B)
1939	Bartali (I)	1958	van Looy (B)	1976	Merckx (B)
1940	Bartali (I)	1959	Poblet (Sp)	1977	Raas (Nl)
1941	Favalli (I)	1960	Privat (F)	1978	de Vlaeminck (B)
1942	Leoni (I)	1961	Poulidor (F)	1979	de Vlaeminck (B)
1943	Cinelli (I)	1962	Daems (B)	1980	Gavazzi (I)
1944–45	not held	1963	Groussard (F)	1981	de Wolf, A. (B)
1946	Coppi (I)	1964	Simpson (GB)	1982	Gomez (F)
1947	Bartali (I)	1965	den Hartog (Nl)	1983	Saronni (I)
1948	Coppi (I)	1966	Merckx (B)	1984	Moser (I)
1949	Coppi (I)	1967	Merckx (B)	1985	Kuiper (Nl)
1950	Bartali (I)	1968	Altig (WG)	1986	Kelly (Ir)
1951	Bobet (F)	1969	Merckx (B)	1987	Maechler (Sw)
1952	Petrucci (I)	1970	Dancelli (I)	1988	Fignon (F)

SPEED RECORD: Eddy Merckx, 44.805 kph in 1967
MOST VICTORIES: Eddy Merckx, 7

Milan-San Remo

Milan-San Remo, often known as the primavera, after the early-blooming primrose flower, is held as close to the first day of spring as possible, given that it is always on a weekend. The gaps of two or three weeks and several hundred miles from Het Volk to Milan-San Remo usually mean a change from wintry to spring weather. However, the conditions are not always as balmy as might be supposed, notably during the first half when the peloton crosses the broad Po Valley from Milan and climbs the 1,745-foot summit of the Turchino Pass.

The history of Milan-San Remo has four distinct phases. Prior to World War I it was truly international, with France the dominant country. During and immediately after the war travel was difficult and when the race was resumed in 1917 it was harder for foreign stars to enter. This led to a domination by Italians that lasted until 1953. Rik van Steenbergen broke the mold in 1954, inaugurating the third phase, a period of 16 years without an Italian victory. Michele Dancelli restored Italian pride in 1970, beginning the fourth phase, when the list of winners has become international again.

After the Turchino, the physical difficulties are minor. From the summit the road descends in 10 miles to Voltri and then hugs the coast of the Ligurian Sea where it is punctuated by a series of short climbs over headlands. To revive flagging interest the organizers added the Poggio detour in 1960, giving the race a last, sinuous climb. The ploy worked very well. But it is ironic that, though the intent was to favor strong riders by adding a final climb, the race has subsequently been won more often than not on the descent from there to San Remo.

The race was founded in 1907 by the managing director of the *Gazzetta dello Sport* and the first prize was 300 lire in gold. There was considerable discussion as to whether the riders would manage to get over the unpaved Turchino. There were 33 entrants. Giovanni Gerbi, an Italian, was first to break clear. By Savona, Gustave Garrigou caught him and Gerbi slowed the pace, allowing Lucien Petit-Breton, riding for the same manufacturer, to join them. (There were no teams in those days, but some riders were employed by bicycle manufacturers.) Gerbi, a poor sprinter, was content to block every move that Garrigou made, hoping for a fair share of the first prize which Petit-Breton eventually won. The second year there were 80 riders and the future was guaranteed.

In 1910 the race entered the realms of the fantastic with the victory of Eugène Christophe. The conditions were so terrible that only 4 of the 71 entrants finished. Three hours and 60 miles after the start Christophe was one minute down on the leaders. Catching them, he learned that Cyrille van Hauwaert and Octave Lapize were further ahead, starting up the Turchino. On the climb Christophe was forced to rest for five minutes to restore some life to his cramped and semi-frozen fingers. Over the top he found van Hauwaert just in front of him, ready to quit. The snow was about eight inches deep, but Christophe, suffering from stomach cramps, struggled through to an inn, where he rested for half an hour. While he was inside, four riders passed. Once warm, Christophe departed, wearing long trousers. He caught the four on the coast, and borrowed a friend's bike for the last 60 miles. He arrived in San Remo in 12:24, the victor. Three of the four caught by Christophe finished, Lapize having disappeared. They were all an hour down at least, with van Hauwaert fourth and last, although a fifth man, Luigi Ganna, struggled in after the race had officially ended.

After World War I came the first rider to be called the *campionissimo*— champion of champions—Costante Girardengo. This Italian won Milan-San Remo six times and crossed the line first on another occasion, but was disqualified for taking the wrong route. Girardengo's record was remarkable, especially since he had almost died of Spanish flu and his manager, believing a survivor of that disease could never race again, had refused to renew his license. Alfredo Binda eventually donned Girardengo's mantle, followed by Gino Bartali.

1946 brought the event for which the whole of sporting Italy had been waiting—the return of Fausto Coppi. Imprisoned in Tunisia and then trapped in southern Italy behind the Allied lines after being released, Coppi eventually made his way home after the German surrender. With no real racing behind him, he had put in 4,000 training miles before reaching Milan.

Seven miles into the race there was a special town prime. Several sprinters maintained their effort after the prize was won and Coppi was onto them like a flash. When the dust settled Coppi and three others were a minute clear. Bartali refused to believe the break was serious, but it grew to four minutes in 30 miles. In the last town before the Turchino, Coppi accelerated to test the others. Only Lucien Teisseire replied. At the foot of the climb they were 6:30 clear. Twice Coppi broke away, allowing Teisseire to rejoin him. The third time, a mile from the summit, he was cheered by hundreds of Italian fans for whom the return of Fausto meant a return to normal. This time he didn't sit up. At the summit Teisseire had lost 100 meters. By Voltri, on the coast, he had lost eight minutes. Coppi covered the 80 miles from Voltri to San Remo at a constant 23 mph, winning despite the desperate attempts by Bartali and the others to join together in the chase. Teisseire placed second at 14 minutes with Mario Ricci just out-sprinting Bartali for third at 18:30.

In 1951 Frenchman Louison Bobet earned an international reputation with his win. But the most famous French ride came in 1958, when René

Being on the route of a major race is a big occasion for a small town. The publicity and business generated can be so great that towns pay to host the start or finish of a stage.

One of the greatest challenges of Milan–San Remo is the 1,745–foot Turchino Pass. This climb, early in the race, often presents wintry conditions that contrast sharply with the warmth and sun of the Ligurian coast.

Privat escaped in a small group on leaving Milan, whittled down the break until he was eventually alone, and was caught and passed with three miles to go. The race lasted six hours, 40 minutes, and he had been in front for six hours, 30 minutes. His consolation came two years later when he won the first Milan-San Remo that included the Poggio.

In 1966 it was Eddy Merckx's turn. The Belgian won six more times between then and 1976, eclipsing the record held by Girardengo since 1928. Three of Merckx's victories were in sprint finishes, and his biggest margin was 30 seconds, in 1971. Merckx probably understood Milan-San Remo better than any modern rider. Apart from his seven victories, he finished in the top 10 only once. It seems that if Merckx and his team judged the race correctly, which they usually did, he won.

In 1970 Dancelli ended the long Italian drought. Typically, Merckx repeatedly organized the chase, almost single-handedly. Dancelli finished alone, six riders slipped away in the closing miles to chase the prizes, and Merckx contented himself by winning the sprint for eighth.

But Merckx learned a lesson. The following year when Roberto Ballini and Bruno Soldi broke away, Merckx sent Joseph Bruyère with them. When Felice Gimondi gave chase, Merckx sent Joseph Spruyt with him. Eventually Merckx himself attacked, taking with him Gianni Motta and Gösta

Petterson. In two miles they had made up almost a minute on Gimondi. With 20 miles to go they reached the break, where Gimondi, in his determination to stay clear, had led for almost 20 miles. The eight were still together at the foot of the Poggio, where Motta took Merckx's wheel. Merckx signalled to Bruyère and Spruyt to take the climb as fast as they could. The line stretched, but didn't break, and Gimondi attacked just before the summit. It was his undoing. Merckx countered immediately, was clear at the top, and won by 30 seconds. Gimondi took the sprint for second with Motta seventh and last, Soldi having been dropped.

Special mention is due Giuseppe Saronni. In 1982, Saronni, like others before him, carried the rainbow jersey of world champion to victory in the Tour of Lombardy. But no Italian world champion had ever gone on to win both Lombardy and Milan-San Remo the following season. Saronni did, and three months later took the Tour of Italy, completing a feat unique in the history of Italian cycling.

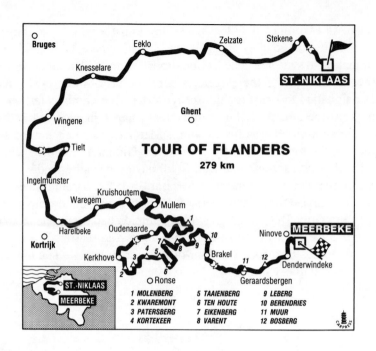

TOUR OF FLANDERS

279 km

1 MOLENBERG   5 TAAIENBERG   9 LEBERG
2 KWAREMONT   6 TEN HOUTE   10 BERENDRIES
3 PATERSBERG   7 EIKENBERG   11 MUUR
4 KORTEKEER   8 VARENT   12 BOSBERG

1913 Deman (B)	**1941** Buysse, A. (B)	**1966** Sels (B)
1914 Buysse, M. (B)	**1942** Schotte (B)	**1967** Zandegu (I)
1915–18 not held	**1943** Buysse, A. (B)	**1968** Godefroot (B)
1919 van Leerberghe (B)	**1944** van Steenbergen (B)	**1969** Merckx (B)
1920 van Hevel (B)	**1945** Grysolle (B)	**1970** Leman (B)
1921 Vermandel (B)	**1946** van Steenbergen (B)	**1971** Dolman (Nl)
1922 de Vos (B)	**1947** Faignaert (B)	**1972** Leman (B)
1923 Suter (Sw)	**1948** Schotte (B)	**1973** Leman (B)
1924 Debaets (B)	**1949** Magni (I)	**1974** Bal (Nl)
1925 Delbecque (B)	**1950** Magni (I)	**1975** Merckx (B)
1926 Verschueren (B)	**1951** Magni (I)	**1976** Planckaert, W. (B)
1927 Debaets (B)	**1952** de Cock (B)	**1977** de Vlaeminck (B)
1928 Mertens (B)	**1953** van Est (Nl)	**1978** Godefroot (B)
1929 Dervaes (B)	**1954** Impanis (B)	**1979** Raas (Nl)
1930 Bonduel (B)	**1955** Bobet (F)	**1980** Pollentier (B)
1931 Gyssels (B)	**1956** Forestier (F)	**1981** Kuiper (Nl)
1932 Gyssels (B)	**1957** de Bruyne (B)	**1982** Martens (B)
1933 Schepers (B)	**1958** Derycke (B)	**1983** Raas (Nl)
1934 Rebry (B)	**1959** van Looy (B)	**1984** Lammerts (Nl)
1935 Duerloo (B)	**1960** de Cabooter (B)	**1985** Vanderaerden (B)
1936 Hardiquest (B)	**1961** Simpson (GB)	**1986** van der Poel (Nl)
1937 d'Hooghe (B)	**1962** van Looy (B)	**1987** Criquielion (B)
1938 de Caluwe (B)	**1963** Foré (B)	**1988** Planckaert, E. (B)
1939 Kaers (B)	**1964** Altig (WG)	
1940 Buysse, A. (B)	**1965** de Roo (Nl)	

SPEED RECORD: Evert Dolman, 43.225 kph in 1971
MOST VICTORIES: Achille Buysse, Fiorenzo Magni, and Eric Leman, 3 each

12   EUROPEAN CYCLING

Tour of Flanders

Uninterrupted by World War II, though held with a considerably impoverished field, the Tour of Flanders has the longest continuous run of any major race. The first major event after Milan-San Remo, it brings riders back from the Mediterranean for the most intensive period of racing in the season, all of it in northern Europe. Held for many years over a course from Ghent to Gentbrugge, a Ghent suburb, the finish of the Tour of Flanders has recently moved to Meerbeke in the same general region. The first half is flat, fast, and often windy, but the second half, like most major Flemish races, turns to the cobbled hills lying south of the Ostende-Brussels highway.

The Tour of Flanders was begun in 1913. It was the brainchild of Karel Steyaert, who worked for *Het Nieuwsblad-Sportswereld* and was sometime manager of the Belgian team in the Tour de France. Steyaert deliberately created a race to cover as much of West Flanders as possible. For several years the newspaper also supported the *Circuit des Regions Flamandes* which followed a route through East Flanders, often ending in Brussels. (Flanders, once a country, is an area of western Belgium and northwest France. It includes the Belgian provinces of East and West Flanders and Flandre, a region and former province of northern France.)

Steyaert's idea, prompted no doubt by a lack of Belgian success in Paris-Brussels, was to create a race that demanded all the qualities a Flemish rider could be expected to display. He succeeded, and was fortunate, in the first two years, to have two significant winners in Paul Deman and Marcel Buysse.

Deman's reputation rests less on his considerable cycling prowess than on his World War I exploits, which earned him medals in Belgium, Britain, and France for bravery. They also earned him a death sentence when he was caught during a secret mission into the Netherlands. Fortunately the armistice was signed just in time to save him.

The second winner, Marcel Buysse, was just as important, though in a different way. French companies were slow to welcome the new race and Buysse, who rode for the Paris-based Alcyon team, had a contract which tied him to races approved by his boss. Although the Tour of Flanders was not among them, Buysse decided that Paris was too far from Ghent for it to matter if he won. He did. Understandably, Alcyon praised his victory rather than disciplining him, consequently encouraging French participation in the race.

But few foreigners have won the Tour of Flanders. From the resumption of the race in 1919 until 1949, Henri Suter of Switzerland was the only non-Belgian to win and what a rumpus he caused. It was said that Suter was so fast a sprinter that, had he ridden the track instead of the road, he would have been world champion many times. Suter's training methods upset race organizer Steyaert. Probably the first to adopt interval training, Suter didn't pound out hundreds of miles on partially paved roads, but went out for relatively short spells, riding alternate kilometers at very high speeds. In competition, he relied on his team and his wits to get him to the finish. Then he won.

One of the more surprising successes was Karel Kaers' in 1939. World road champion five years before, Kaers had turned to the track and only occasionally entered a road race. Then he decided to win Paris-Roubaix, using the first part of the Tour of Flanders for training. To the consternation of his manager, Kaers instructed friends to bring his car to the top of the Kwaremont—some 140 km from the start—so he could quit there and drive home in comfort. Kaers' manager went to the summit to find and remove the car. Imagine his feelings when Kaers and his training partner appeared, a minute clear of the field.

Despite the roar of the crowd, Kaers sought his car. Unable to spot it, he decided to go as far as the next climb. Meanwhile Edward Vissers and Romain Maes came up and, picking up the pace, dropped Kaers' partner. On the last climb Kaers was 20 meters back, and there was still no car to be seen. Furious, he set about rejoining Vissers and Maes, and then beat them in the sprint 30 miles later.

One of the most important steps in the internationalization of cycling was the creation of the Desgranges-Colombo Challenge in 1948. This precursor to the Pernod competition was awarded on the basis of points won in the top classics of the day. In order to have a chance at the trophy and cash prize, riders were obliged to travel more extensively than before, and many did.

Fiorenzo Magni was one. Little respected in his native Italy where Gino Bartali and Fausto Coppi were still heroes, Magni entered the Tour of Flanders in 1949 and won a tumultuous sprint. The following year he won alone by 2:06 and in 1951 he was 5:35 clear at the finish. Flemish domination of the race was finally broken.

The first French victory should have gone to Louison Bobet in 1952. Winner of both Italian classics the year before, Bobet was intent on showing the world that he was the greatest. In Flanders that year he almost certainly was, but Bobet was never one to listen to advice, and that may have cost him the win. Riding confidently, he proposed to attack on the Kwaremont, a long way from the finish. Ignoring warnings to wait until the final climb—the Mur de Grammont—he attacked and broke clear. Over the Mur he was still away, but his lead was beginning to fade when he punctured. There were only seven miles to go, but Bobet had taken too much out of himself. Instead of winning he finished sixth, 1:20 down.

In 1955 Bobet returned to Flanders wearing the rainbow jersey of world champion. Early attacks came and went, but as far as the Mur de Grammont Bobet refused to turn a pedal in anger. At Grammont he attacked and split the field completely, taking with him only three, including Rik van Steenbergen, reputedly the fastest road sprinter in the world. The four stayed together for the final sprint, where Bobet won with ease, but the race was not yet over.

Injury is one of the greatest risks of bicycle racing. This crash was in the 1983 Tour of Flanders. On narrow roads like this one over the Koppenberg, such accidents not only stop the riders involved, but also hold up those behind.

Bobet's teammate Karel Debaere was fifth, down 22 seconds. On van Steenbergen's recommendation he contested the result, since the four leaders had climbed over a closed railroad crossing gate. Bobet knew very well that he and his companions had been under the surveillance of police commissaires at the gate and he didn't deign to put in a counterclaim. Sure enough, the complaint was rejected and Bobet's victory confirmed.

The Tour of Flanders had a curious and significant finish in 1961, when Tom Simpson became the first British victor. Over the last few miles the survivors of an earlier break split up, leaving Simpson and Nino Defilippis in the lead. As they approached the line, where fast Defilippis could be expected to win comfortably, Simpson appeared to launch his sprint too early. Defilippis went with him and, seeing a banner in front, jumped away from Simpson, one arm raised in victory. But Simpson knew exactly where the line was and continued his sprint to the true banner, leaving a bemused Defilippis to complain bitterly, but in vain.

One of the most spectacular post-war victories was that of Eddy Merckx in 1969. Born in Brussels, Merckx was not Flemish. Walter Godefroot was the idol of Ghent and Roger de Vlaeminck was next in popularity. Although Merckx was beginning to dominate world cycling, he had yet to ride the Tour de France. His reputation, though considerable, was not yet unmatchable. In 1967 he had been well and truly worked over in Flanders by the Italian duo of Felice Gimondi and Dino Zandegu. In 1968 he had been unable to cope with the masterful ability of Walter Godefroot. By 1969 he was determined to show that he could conquer Flanders.

Signs were not propitious. Gimondi and Zandegu were there again with a strong team. The Flandria team under Briek Schotte had been instructed to stop Merckx at all costs. And most Flemish riders—there were 70 of them—were prepared to overlook team loyalty and band together against the parvenu who threatened them. They would rather see a foreigner win than a rider from the wrong part of Belgium.

A raging blizzard at the start turned into a fine rain which left the cobbles glistening and treacherous. Merckx decided to force a confrontation relatively early, in the hope of tiring those who had recently ridden a stage race. Attacking ferociously before the Kwaremont he split the field in two. Between the Kwaremont and the Mur de Grammont, Merckx's Faema team kept up a relentless pace. The second attack came before the Mur, just as some of the victims of the first were struggling back.

At the top of the most famous hill in Flanders, Merckx was clear, with Gimondi chasing and also ahead of the bunch. The team cars had been routed around Grammont to avoid the narrow, cobbled hill where 20,000 people were standing in the rain. When the support vehicles rejoined the race with 50 miles to go, Merckx was advised to cut his effort and let the leaders form a break with him, or at least to wait for Gimondi. Merckx wanted no advice. Over the Valkenberg and the Kasteelstraat his lead increased, but Gimondi kept up the chase. At the finish Merckx won by 5:36, and Basso took the sprint for third at 8:08. Merckx later described this victory as one of the most satisfying of his career. Credit must be given to Gimondi for his persistence. In terms of sheer class, Gimondi was probably equal to Fausto Coppi, but Coppi didn't have Merckx to ride against for most of his career.

The six years before Merckx won again were marked by the triple success of Eric Leman. He won three times in four years, every time in a sprint, and every time with Merckx alongside him in the lead bunch. But it may not have mattered to Merckx, who was building his reputation in the Tour de France.

A statue of Karel Steyaert stands at the summit of the Kwaremont, which was resurfaced to provide a smooth climb to the top. In 1975 the organizers made a change in the route that met with Merckx's approval, taking the field up a narrow track which emerged in front of the statue. It was there that Merckx attacked, taking Frans Verbeeck with him. Merckx led the way over every hill. There were suggestions that Verbeeck had agreed not to sprint if Merckx towed him to second, but both riders denied this. It didn't matter, since Merckx attacked with three miles to go, beating Verbeeck by 30 seconds and the bunch by 5:02. At the finish Verbeeck had to be helped from his bike.

The last great confrontation was in 1977. Merckx attacked before the first hill to such effect that only de Vlaeminck and Freddy Maertens were able to follow. Then de Vlaeminck punctured and had to chase for 15 miles to reach the leaders. On the dreadful Koppenberg, Maertens smashed his bike and had to change and chase after the other two. On the Varentberg, Merckx was dropped and retired.

Then came the news that Maertens would be disqualified for an illegal bike change. He had led the race for 10 miles, with de Vlaeminck refusing to come out from his sheltered position. Now de Vlaeminck was apparently alone. Maertens continued to relay him all the way to the finish, but didn't bother sprinting.

Two hours later the race jury awarded second to Maertens, but the Belgian Cycling Federation disqualified him because his replacement bike was given to him by a member of the Flandria organization who was planted there for that very purpose. Finally came the news that Maertens' urine sample had revealed traces of a forbidden substance.

Since 1977 Belgium and the Netherlands have shared the victories equally, but the great days of Merckx and the Flandria opposition have disappeared and the Tour of Flanders is still awaiting its new hero.

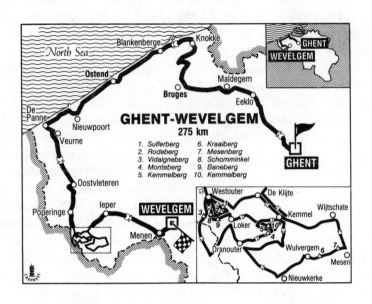

1945	van Eename (B)	1960	Aerenhouts (B)	1975	Maertens (B)
1946	Sterckx (B)	1961	Aerenhouts (B)	1976	Maertens (B)
1947	de Simpelaere (B)	1962	van Looy (B)	1977	Hinault (B)
1948	Ollivier (B)	1963	Beheyt (B)	1978	van den Haute (B)
1949	Kint (B)	1964	Anquetil (F)	1979	Moser (I)
1950	Schotte (B)	1965	de Pauw (B)	1980	Lubberding (NI)
1951	Rosseel (B)	1966	van Springel (B)	1981	Raas (NI)
1952	Impanis (B)	1967	Merckx (B)	1982	Hoste (B)
1953	Impanis (B)	1968	Godefroot (B)	1983	van Vliet, L. (NI)
1954	Graf (Sw)	1969	Vekemans (B)	1984	Bontempi (I)
1955	Schotte (B)	1970	Merckx (B)	1985	Vanderaerden (B)
1956	van Looy (B)	1971	Pintens (B)	1986	Bontempi (I)
1957	van Looy (B)	1972	Swerts (B)	1987	van Vliet, T. (NI)
1958	Foré (B)	1973	Merckx (B)	1988	Kelly (Ir)
1959	van Daele (B)	1974	Hoban (GB)		

SPEED RECORD: Guido Bontempi, 44.776 kph in 1986
MOST VICTORIES: Eddy Merckx, Rik van Looy, 3 each

Ghent-Wevelgem

In 1934 Georges Matthys organized the first Ghent-Wevelgem for juniors. Starting in 1936 the race was for semi-professionals. In 1945 it was opened to professionals and the winner was Robert van Eename, which seems appropriate since he had won twice as an independent. Matthys' claimed intention was to attract the highest quality field possible. He has succeeded outstandingly, with a record of 258 starters in 1985, beaten only by the all-time record of 260 in Milan-San Remo.

Ghent-Wevelgem, sponsored now by *Het Laatste Nieuws*, another Belgian newspaper, is similar in profile to Het Volk and the Tour of Flanders, though less severe. It starts into the prevailing wind, traveling west from Ghent to the coast, which it follows almost to the French border. It then follows the border south to Poperinge, where the hilly section starts. There are usually five or six classified climbs, some of them ridden two or three times, then a flat run of some 30 miles to the finish. Matthys points out that while the race is often criticized as being designed for sprinters, there have been only three mass sprint wins in its history.

Despite its popularity with foreign riders, Ghent-Wevelgem was dominated for a long time by Belgians, whose victories were punctuated only by the surprising success of Swiss Rolf Graf in 1954. It was another 10 years to the next foreign victory, and an amazing one it was. The story is told in *Anquetil* written by Jacques Anquetil's wife and Pierre Chany (Hatier, 1971). Anquetil was near the back of the bunch, alongside a Belgian. Anquetil asked how far it was to the finish and was told just over two miles. "This was the signal. He jumped from the back and surprised all the Belgian roadmen-sprinters, including (Rik) van Looy and his red guards." In fact, Anquetil won by one second and, had the line been 100 yards further, he would have been closer to 50th than first.

Ten more years passed and, again, victory could hardly have been more surprising. The GAN-Mercier team was in fine form, with Joop Zoetemelk winning Paris-Nice and Cees Bal taking the Tour of Flanders, and with

Raymond Poulidor on board. Then there was their rival, Eddy Merckx, a three-time winner like van Looy. Merckx needed only one more victory to be the record-holder, and the Flemish riders were out to stop him.

Nothing significant happened by the Kemmelberg, climbed twice, once in each direction. Roger de Vlaeminck led over the top the first time, ahead of Merckx and Frans Verbeeck, with Verbeeck taking the honors the second time. The bunch had split, but the gaps were not large and Barry Hoban, about 200 yards down at the summit, was paced back by teammate Poulidor, who was returning the help often given him in the Tour de France. Then Herman van Springel jumped and Poulidor fetched him back. The top Belgian sprinters were all at the front waiting for the finish, but Poulidor sat on every attempt to break away.

The lead bunch approached the line intact. Merckx was there with Roger Swerts to lead him out. De Vlaeminck and others were there, too. Eric Leman jumped too early. Walter Godefroot took the wrong wheel and found himself balked. As they neared the finish it seemed that Merckx and de Vlaeminck would fight it out, but suddenly a GAN-Mercier jersey appeared between the two leaders and, with an elbow-stretching lunge, Hoban took the win.

Being on the finish line side of a passing train can often make the difference between victory and defeat. Some riders have even climbed over a closed gate—in many countries an illegal maneuver that can lead to disqualification.

The most significant foreign victory took place in 1977, over a different course than usual. The field was smashed on the dreaded Koppenberg, followed by the Kwaremont and the Kruisberg. Seven men broke away and built up a four-minute lead, but it was wiped out on the Kemmelberg, climbed twice as usual. With 20 miles to go, another seven emerged from the new lead group to contest the Mont Rouge. They, too, were caught, but not before Bernard Hinault jumped away alone. After surviving the hilliest Ghent-Wevelgem ever he time trialed his way to a 1:24 victory. Daniel Schamps, reporting the race for *International Cycle Sport*, asked "could France have a new Anquetil?" Yes indeed—and a lot more.

1896 Fischer, J. (G)		
1897 Garin (F)		
1898 Garin (F)		
1899 Champion (F)		
1900 Bouhours (F)		
1901 Lesna (F)		
1902 Lesna (F)		
1903 Aucouturier (F)		
1904 Aucouturier (F)		
1905 Trousselier (F)		
1906 Cornet (F)		
1907 Passérieu (F)		
1908 van Hauwaert (B)		
1909 Lapize (F)		
1910 Lapize (F)		
1911 Lapize (F)		
1912 Crupelandt (F)		
1913 Faber (L)		
1914 Crupelandt (F)		
1915–18 not held		
1919 Pélissier, H. (F)		
1920 Deman (B)		
1921 Pélissier, H. (F)		
1922 de Jonghe (B)		
1923 Suter (Sw)		
1924 van Hevel (B)		
1925 Sellier (B)		
1926 Delbecque (B)		
1927 Ronsse (B)		
1928 Leducq (F)		
1929 Meunier (B)		

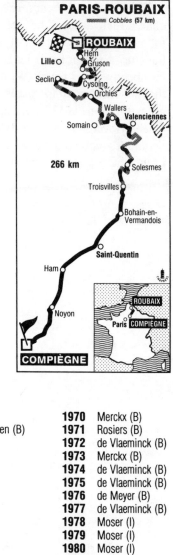

1930 Vervaecke (B)	**1951** Bevilacqua (I)	**1970** Merckx (B)
1931 Rebry (B)	**1952** van Steenbergen (B)	**1971** Rosiers (B)
1932 Gyssels (B)	**1953** Derycke (B)	**1972** de Vlaeminck (B)
1933 Maes, S. (B)	**1954** Impanis (B)	**1973** Merckx (B)
1934 Rebry (B)	**1955** Forestier (F)	**1974** de Vlaeminck (B)
1935 Rebry (B)	**1956** Bobet (F)	**1975** de Vlaeminck (B)
1936 Speicher (F)	**1957** de Bruyne (B)	**1976** de Meyer (B)
1937 Rossi (I)	**1958** van Daele (B)	**1977** de Vlaeminck (B)
1938 Storme (B)	**1959** Foré (B)	**1978** Moser (I)
1939 Masson, E. Jr. (B)	**1960** Cerami (B)	**1979** Moser (I)
1940–42 not held	**1961** van Looy (B)	**1980** Moser (I)
1943 Kint (B)	**1962** van Looy (B)	**1981** Hinault (F)
1944 de Simpelaere (B)	**1963** Daems (B)	**1982** Raas (NI)
1945 Maye (F)	**1964** Post (NI)	**1983** Kuiper (NI)
1946 Claes (B)	**1965** van Looy (B)	**1984** Kelly (Ir)
1947 Claes (B)	**1966** Gimondi (I)	**1985** Madiot (F)
1948 van Steenbergen (B)	**1967** Janssen (NI)	**1986** Kelly (Ir)
1949 Mahe (F) & Coppi, S. (I)	**1968** Merckx (B)	**1987** Vanderaerden (B)
1950 Coppi, F. (I)	**1969** Godefroot (B)	**1988** de Mol (B)

SPEED RECORD: Peter Post, 45.129 kph in 1964
MOST VICTORIES: Roger de Vlaeminck, 4

Paris-Roubaix

Bordeaux-Paris had been run five times and Paris-Brest-Paris once when three northern Frenchmen had the idea of using the already-popular Roubaix velodrome to house the finish of a race from Paris in 1896. Pacing machines were allowed and the eventual entry list included 118 riders. The bookmakers made Josef Fischer the favorite, ahead of Maurice Garin and Paul Guignard.

In the forest of St. Germain, Arthur Linton forged ahead, paced by his brother. At Beauvais he was four minutes up on the favorites. By Amiens, Fischer had joined him and they were six minutes ahead of Garin, when a dog brought Linton down. Fischer continued alone and Garin overtook Linton, who continued despite multiple cuts and abrasions. Eventually a Dane, Charles Meyer, passed both Linton and Garin to take second, 26 seconds behind Fischer, with Garin third at 0:28 and Linton fourth at 0:42. The race was so successful that it was agreed to hold it annually on Easter, which is why it is known as *la Pascale*.

Pacing by bicycles lasted another year, cars were used for two years, and bicycle pacing was restored until 1910. It made little difference to Octave Lapize. Employing no pacers and riding his first major race as a professional, Lapize stayed with the pace and found himself on the Roubaix track with Louis Trousselier and Jules Masselis. There were several laps to cover, but the trio had barely finished the first lap when Cyrille van Hauwaert arrived, having been delayed by a puncture. The thousands of Belgian spectators went wild with delight as van Hauwaert made up half a lap, but then he ran out of steam. In the final sprint, Lapize easily beat van Hauwaert who was highly indignant at being fourth, one lap down.

Lapize won again in another sprint the next year. He took his hat trick in 1911, when no pacing was allowed, finishing alone by more than three minutes. Lapize was one of the stars who didn't survive World War I, being killed in a dogfight in 1917.

The race was suspended in 1915 because of the war. When it resumed in

1919 the victory went to Henri Pélissier and the following year to Paul Deman, a war hero. But Pélissier hadn't yet had his last word.

In 1921 Pélissier and his brother Francis refused to sign an agreement that fixed the rate of remuneration and set riders' contracts for all races for two years. Instead, they found a small firm to pay their costs for Paris-Roubaix, where they competed against 130 contracted riders. Word went out that a Pélissier must not win. However, when the first major break came they were both there, with 20 rivals around them. Already the odds had been considerably reduced. The cobbles and punctures took their toll until the lead group was reduced to five, including the brothers. Eventually only René Vermandel was left with them. The Pélissiers adopted a classic maneuver, separating to opposite sides of the road and attacking in turn. Every time one attacked, Vermandel replied, but it couldn't last. Finally Henri broke him and went on to win alone, with Francis taking the sprint for second.

With the power of the pact between manufacturers and riders limited if not broken, the way was open. The largest field ever assembled for Paris-Roubaix started in 1923 and accounts of the finish vary. One newspaper claimed that the final sprint was contested by 156, which must make it the biggest sprint finish in any classic. Victory went, not surprisingly, to the Swiss sprinter, Henri Suter. Then the Belgians took over the race for several years, helped by a little luck.

In 1930 Jean Maréchal, a 20-year-old French track star, escaped with Julien Vervaecke. They worked well together until Vervaecke was ordered to stop cooperating. Twice Vervaecke attacked suddenly and twice Maréchal pulled him back. The second time was only four miles from the finish and, as Maréchal caught Vervaecke and tried to go past, there was a tangling of limbs and Vervaecke fell. Maréchal went on to win, but was demoted to second place that evening when the Alcyon team management protested on behalf of Vervaecke, who was one of their riders.

Four years later it was Roger Lapébie's turn to be disappointed. Rules had been changed to allow damaged equipment to be replaced during the race by equipment from another rider, from the team director, or even, in an emergency, from a spectator. Inside the zone where changes were allowed, and close enough to the finish for it to be a serious problem, Lapébie punctured. The only other rider with him was Gaston Rebry, who had won in 1931. With no team car at hand, Lapébie was lucky enough to find a spectator with a bike of more or less the right size, though certainly not a racing model. Lapébie caught and dropped Rebry, finishing alone, but was disqualified for an allegedly illegal change of bicycle. Rebry completed his hat trick in 1935.

Belgian domination continued until 1949. That year three riders held a slight lead at the approach to the velodrome, where they were misdirected. Unable to find the correct way in, they had to carry their bikes through a turnstile to resume the race, with André Mahe beating the other two. Unfortunately for him, the peloton had already arrived and Serse Coppi had been first over the line. The officials decided to award both men first place, one of the few instances of a dead heat in classics history.

There were no such errors the following year when Serse's brother, Fausto Coppi, attacked at a feeding station and burned off all but one of his companions immediately. He attacked and attacked until he got rid of Maurice Diot and went on to win alone, leaving Diot to declare that he himself had won, Coppi being *hors concours*—beyond competition.

It wasn't until 1956 that Louison Bobet satisfied his public by winning Paris-Roubaix, ignoring medical instructions not to race until the scar of an operation had healed. Six riders survived the usual cobbled chaos to approach Roubaix together. On the track Bernard Gauthier jumped first, obliging Rik van Steenbergen to chase. Alfred de Bruyne came off van Steenbergen's wheel, but Bobet was ready and swept past to win by a margin comfortable enough to allow him to cross the line with both arms raised.

The last 30 years have seen many fine exploits, but four men have dominated. The earliest was Rik van Looy, an outstanding rider on the difficult and often dangerous cobbles that the organizers are constantly having to seek out, as road improvements render another bit of the course inappropriate. But before van Looy achieved his first win, two others had been particularly unfortunate.

Jacques Anquetil hated Paris-Roubaix, but knew that he was expected to make an effort to win it at least once. That effort came in 1958. Attacking early, he put two minutes between himself and the van Looy group. Attacking again on the cobbles (which he detested), he reduced the lead group to a handful. With 10 miles to go they were down to four, with Anquetil in complete charge and looking certain to win. Then he punctured. The wheel was quickly replaced and Anquetil caught the remaining trio in three miles, but those 25 seconds taken to replace the wheel were enough to allow the bunch to catch up.

In 1960 came Eurovision coverage for the first time. Viewers marveled at the daring of a young unknown who, it was later claimed, based his attack at a railroad crossing upon advance knowledge of the times when trains were due. He had 50 miles to ride as the gates closed behind him and he lasted 45 of them before being caught. This was Tom Simpson's first great ride.

It's not for nothing that Paris-Roubaix is known as the Hell of the North. Sometimes it's muddy and sometimes it's dusty, but the narrow, dirt roads and rough, cobbled tracks always take their toll on riders and often on the press corps, too. Above, four-time winner Roger de Vlaeminck (right), Ferdi van den Haute (left), and Ludo Peeters (center) in the 1981 race. Below, a rider signals his team car for help.

The next two years van Looy took the two of his three victories. He should have won again in 1963, having instructed Armand Desmet to lead him out in the sprint. However, two of his rivals boxed in Desmet, who was unable to pull out and let his captain through. The winner, Emil Daems, was innocent of any complicity in a maneuver that, while not illegal, was unethical.

Peter Post won in 1964, setting a race record of 28.03 mph which was also the record for any classic for many years. In 1965 van Looy completed his triple. It should have been four (or five) in 1967, as he prepared to overhaul Jan Janssen on the Roubaix track, only to have a rival's hand grasp his jersey and hold him back.

The reign of Eddy Merckx began in 1968. Merckx, who also won three times, was not as outstanding over the cobbles as van Looy or Roger de Vlaeminck. But he was incredibly thorough in checking his equipment. He never punctured because of a faulty tire; his saddle height was adjusted during the race to suit different conditions; his gloves were specially padded to withstand the shaking of the cobbles. But even Merckx could do nothing, in 1972, about de Vlaeminck.

A former world cyclocross champion, de Vlaeminck had no fear of the cobbles. He was also a good enough roadman to win races where every road was as smooth as a well-maintained track. Twelve were in front when de Vlaeminck attacked, followed by Merckx, who was forced by injuries to watch his rival ride away. De Vlaeminck won by 1:57. He took the race again in 1974, by 57 seconds.

But in 1975 de Vlaeminck failed to escape, finding himself in a group of 10, eventually cut to four by Merckx's efforts. Then Merckx punctured. It took him two miles to catch the trio. As he closed on them, he switched to the other side of the road to jump straight past. Marc de Meyer was watching and shouted a warning, prompting de Vlaeminck to react just in time and to go on to a narrow victory on the track. De Vlaeminck's fourth win came in 1977. Although he was in poor form the week before, he simply rode away from Freddy Maertens, who had been winning all season.

Of 14 starts, de Vlaeminck failed to finish only once. His positions, from 1969, were: 5th, 7th, 2nd, 1st, 7th, 1st, 1st, 3rd, 1st, 2nd, 2nd, dnf, 2nd, and 6th. With 13 top-seven showings in 14 seasons, de Vlaeminck is likely to remain the archetypal Paris-Roubaix rider for many years to come.

Yet de Vlaeminck was challenged almost immediately by a most unlikely opponent, whose victory he aided. Although Francesco Moser was the reigning world road champion, several of his rivals spoke disparagingly about his championship win in Venezuela. In addition, Italy had a rising new star in Giuseppe Saronni. In 1978 four riders—de Vlaeminck and Moser of the Sanson team, Maertens, and Jan Raas—were together with 20 miles to go. When Moser took off alone de Vlaeminck neutralized Maertens and Raas, whom he then comfortably outsprinted for second, even though they were allegedly the fastest pair in the world. Moser repeated the following year, pursuiting his way to a 40-second solo victory with de Vlaeminck again second.

Moser and de Vlaeminck were there again in 1980, this time with Dietrich Thurau and Gilbert Duclos-Lasalle at 20 miles to go. When de Vlaeminck punctured Moser made his move with Duclos-Lasalle on his wheel. In the next 15 miles Duclos-Lasalle punctured twice and fell once but never gave up the chase. On the track Moser equalled the feat of Octave Lapize by taking his third win in a row.

In 1981 it could have been four in a row for Moser, or a fifth for de Vlaeminck. Six reached the track together, Moser and de Vlaeminck among them. Bernard Hinault, determined to let nobody take a flier, had led for the last two miles into Roubaix. He let Hennie Kuiper take the lead on the track with a lap and a half left, but came past him with 400 yards still to go. On the back straight Hinault fought off an attack from de Meyer and off the last bend he resisted de Vlaeminck's attempt to get past. Nobody could have beaten Hinault that day—not even the great French track sprinter Daniel Morelon.

Hinault, like Anquetil, detested Paris-Roubaix but knew that the French public expected him to win it once. Some writers claimed that Hinault was a poor sprinter. Don't believe it. Hinault, in a position to launch the long sprint that he preferred, was the fastest finisher in the world. The men he beat on the track that day had won Paris-Roubaix for the previous seven years.

Since then only Sean Kelly seems to have a chance of matching Moser or de Vlaeminck, having won twice. In 1984, with Alain Bondue and Gregor Braun out in front for much of the race, Kelly split the field by his first attack. He took Rudy Rogiers with him in his second attack, caught and dropped the two leaders, and then outsprinted Rogiers for the win. Two years later it was a similar story. Kelly launched the vital attack, this time taking three others whom he dispatched without difficulty in Roubaix. Long breaks rarely succeed in Paris-Roubaix. In 1988, when a group of riders disappeared up the road after only 20 miles they were allowed their freedom. By the start of the cobbles the break had gained a 10-minute lead, but the leaders fell one by one, from punctures or just because they had weakened. Dirk de Mol, Thomas Wegmüller, and Stephen Joho—none well-known in pro cycling—remained in front. When the reaction came, it was too late. Laurent Fignon and Marc Sergeant caught Joho, but de Mol and Wegmüller had broken away, not to be seen until Roubaix. At the finish Wegmüller was hampered by a plastic bag that got caught in his derailleur, giving de Mol an easy sprint win and his first major victory.

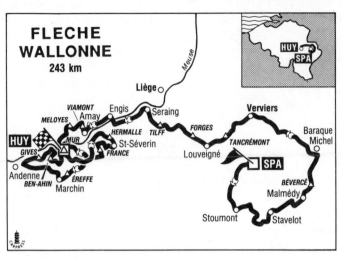

FLECHE WALLONNE
243 km

1936 de Meersman (B)	**1955** Ockers (B)	**1973** Dierickx (B)
1937 Braeckeveldt (B)	**1956** van Genechten (B)	**1974** Verbeeck (B)
1938 Masson, E. Jr. (B)	**1957** Impanis (B)	**1975** Dierickx (B)
1939 Delathouwer (B)	**1958** van Steenbergen (B)	**1976** Zoetemelk (Nl)
1940 not held	**1959** Hoevenaers (B)	**1977** Moser (I)
1941 Grysolle (B)	**1960** Cerami (B)	**1978** Laurent (F)
1942 Thys, K. (B)	**1961** Vannitsen (B)	**1979** Hinault (F)
1943 Kint (B)	**1962** de Wolf, H. (B)	**1980** Saronni (I)
1944 Kint (B)	**1963** Poulidor (F)	**1981** Willems (B)
1945 Kint (B)	**1964** Desmet, G. (B)	**1982** Beccia (I)
1946 Keteleer (B)	**1965** Poggiali (I)	**1983** Hinault (F)
1947 Sterckx (B)	**1966** Dancelli (I)	**1984** Andersen (D)
1948 Camellini (I)	**1967** Merckx (B)	**1985** Criquielion (B)
1949 van Steenbergen (B)	**1968** van Looy (B)	**1986** Fignon (F)
1950 Coppi (I)	**1969** Huysmans (B)	**1987** Leclercq (F)
1951 Kubler (Sw)	**1970** Merckx (B)	**1988** Gölz (WG)
1952 Kubler (Sw)	**1971** de Vlaeminck (B)	
1953 Ockers (B)	**1972** Merckx (B)	
1954 Derycke (B)		

SPEED RECORD: Bernard Hinault, 39.876 kph in 1979*
MOST VICTORIES: Eddy Merckx, Marcel Kint, 3 each

* Daniel Willems won at 41.260 in 1981 over an amended course without hills. The Pernod organization downgraded the race in 1982 and *Vélo* cites Hinault as the recordholder over the traditional course.

Flèche Wallonne

With the Flèche Wallonne the classics enter another world. All the earlier races except Milan-San Remo are held in relatively flat country, where the climbs are short, vicious, and usually cobbled. The Belgian Ardennes, by contrast, is an area of rounded, tree-covered hills. The climbs are long and winding here, but still steep, at times.

The Flèche Wallonne and its sister race, Liège-Bastogne-Liège, have a checkered history. The Pernod organization used to award 60 points to the winner of most classics, but these were considered 35-point races. For a while they were run on successive days to constitute the *Weekend Ardennais*, which had an overall classification and prize list. Then they were separated and held on the Thursday and Sunday after Paris-Roubaix, each coming first in alternate years. For several years now they've been held in a fixed order.

Slightly easier, the Flèche Wallonne is the midweek race. It was founded in 1936 by *Les Sports*, another Belgian newspaper. Its route originally linked Tournai and Liège, two cities in the Walloon region of Belgium, in a more or less straight line. Hence the name Flèche Wallonne—Walloon Arrow. Nowadays, the route varies from year to year. Unlike Liège-Bastogne-Liège, an out-and-back race, the Flèche Wallonne usually links two towns in or near the Ardennes, and recent editions have finished in Huy. These two classics are unique in being the only ones where the record speed has not yet reached 25 mph.

Flèche Wallonne didn't attract a truly international field until after World War II, the earlier editions being largely a settling of scores between Flemish and Walloon riders. (The Dutch-speaking Flemish of western Belgium are great rivals of the French-speaking Walloons from the southern and southeastern part of the nation.) But the arrival of Fausto Coppi in 1949 brought two sensational races.

Pino Cerami, also Italian, was the only man left from a break when Coppi attacked. They quickly reached an agreement. Cerami was first over

31

all the hills with Coppi, who knew that he could ride away whenever he chose, but was content to have a companion to share the pace. Unfortunately for them, Rik van Steenbergen and Edward Peters managed to find shelter behind a car while breaking away. Innocently, it was later claimed, the car paced them up to the lead and van Steenbergen went on to win. Cerami's greatest years came much later when, as a naturalized Belgian, he won Paris-Roubaix at the age of 38.

The following year Coppi used his favorite tactic, attacking at the feed station and riding away from the field. He won by five minutes, to the joy of the Walloon crowd that felt justice had been done.

Strangely, Coppi was not there in 1951 for one of the great races of all time. Gino Bartali, Louison Bobet, Ferdi Kubler, and Jean Robic broke away. The four, all past or future winners of the Tour de France, attacked each other mile after mile with nobody weakening. On every climb one would gain a few yards, to be hauled back by the other three. This went on for 90 miles. Contemporary newspapers claimed that Bartali launched the final sprint with a mile to go. At the line it was Kubler, followed by Bartali, Robic, and, three lengths back, Bobet.

Kubler, dubbed the Swiss Cowboy because of his fondness for Stetsons, won Liège-Bastogne-Liège the next day and repeated the double the following year. Only Stan Ockers and Eddy Merckx have since won both races in the same year.

Rik van Looy leads a group that includes, from left, Jan Janssen, Jos Huysmans, and José Samyn in the 1968 Flèche Wallonne. Van Looy won the race, a victory that made him the only rider to win the eight orthodox classics.

Clowning for photographers is a popular diversion during slow stages or in the early miles of a long event, as Bert Oosterbosch demonstrates.

Van Steenbergen's first classic win was in the 1949 Flèche Wallonne. His last was in the same event in 1958. That year Rik van Looy had just taken Paris-Brussels, his first classic, and though van Steenbergen held the world title, the Belgian press was hailing Rik II as the new champion. In the Flèche Wallonne van Steenbergen chased and caught the lead bunch, punctured, and caught them again. He lost 100 yards on the last hill, recovered, and sprinted with such power that he won by three seconds. According to Theo Mathy in *Vingt-Cinq Ans de Cyclisme* (Arts et Voyages, 1972), as he dismounted, his first words were "The 'Old Man' is still around." Van Looy finished five minutes later.

Van Looy's day was to come. No rider has ever won the 10 original classics, and no rider had ever won the eight orthodox ones until 1968. When he started the Flèche Wallonne that year, Van Looy had won seven. Finding himself clear with one minor rider, van Looy fought for 50 miles against a chasing trio. The three—Jan Janssen, Felice Gimondi, and Herman van Springel—respectively won the Tour de France, Tour of Spain, and Pernod Trophy later that season. At the line van Looy had 15 yards to spare. The chasers, led still by the famous trio, were more than a minute down on the man whose classic record remains unique.

If this was triumph, the next year was farce. Nine riders, including Eddy Merckx and five of his Flandria team rivals, were away together. Every move that Merckx made was countered by one of the others, yet none had the courage to attack. When the attack came it was from Jos Huysmans of a third team and, as Merckx sat there laughing, the Flandria riders let Huysmans ride away to a 10-second victory. Revenge for Merckx was not to be delayed for long, as Liège-Bastogne-Liège would prove.

Bernard Hinault's 1979 victory in the Flèche Wallonne was one of those that make nonsense of the claim that he couldn't sprint. Five riders had been almost two minutes clear when, with 20 miles left, Hinault led the chase up the Wall of Thuin. The leaders were caught on the next climb and a new bunch of 20 emerged. Bernt Johanssen attacked with three miles to go. Giuseppe Saronni was on his wheel, followed by Hinault. When they were clear Saronni must have imagined himself the winner. He was the fastest roadman in the world and he had Hinault to protect him. Hinault did just that, but as the trio rounded the last corner for an uphill sprint, it was Hinault who jumped away to win in style.

Ironically it was another Swede, Sven-Ake Nilsson, who made the final

Climbs in many of the spring classics are sometimes so steep that riders push or carry their bikes.

break in 1980 for Saronni, who went with him and won comfortably, with Hinault third at 1:40. But Hinault got revenge. In 1983 the race was promenading toward a sprint finish when Hinault attacked up the Wall of Huy and dropped Saronni from the lead bunch. Thirty riders had started the climb together. At the top there were six, and Hinault had no difficulty beating the others in the eventual sprint, with the American Jonathan Boyer fifth.

It's amazing what a world championship rainbow jersey can do to a rider. It made all the difference to Tom Simpson in the 1965 Tour of Lombardy, it gave Saronni a unique place in Italian racing history, and it turned Claude Criquielion into a different rider altogether.

Criquielion was one of those Belgian stage race riders likely to finish in the top 10, but unlikely to win. But in 1984 he took advantage of a lethargic field to win the world championship. He lined up for the 1985 Flèche Wallonne with a rainbow jersey on his shoulders, one of only three Walloon riders among the scores of Flemish in the race. The race was three-quarters over when the first major attack took place. Five, including Criquielion, emerged over the Wall of Huy. He attacked, dislodging Jef Lieckens. Then he shook off Acacio da Silva and Laurent Fignon. Only Moreno Argentin remained and he vanished with 10 miles to go, during which Criquielion gained 1:49 in a style which earned him comparison with Eddy Merckx. In six Ardennes races following his world title, Criquielion finished 1st, 2nd, 4th, 4th, 2nd, and 3rd. He still hadn't won a major stage race, but his rainbow jersey had turned him into a fine rider of classics.

1894	Houa (B)				
1912	Verschoore (B)				
1913–18	not held				
1919	de Vos (B)				
1920	Scieur (B)				
1921	Mottiat (B)				
1922	Mottiat (B)				
1923	Vermandel (B)				
1924	Vermandel (B)				

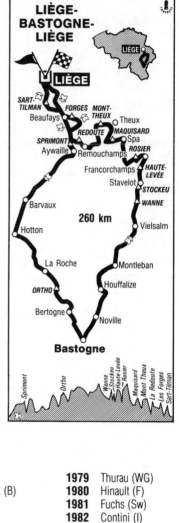

1930 Buse (G)
1931 Schepers (B)
1932 Houyoux (B)
1933 Gardier (B)
1934 Herckenrath (B)
1935 Schepers (B)
1936 Beckaert (B)
1937 Meulenberg (B)
1938 Deloor, G. (B)
1939 Ritserveldt (B)
1940–42 not held
1943 Depoorter (B)
1944 not held
1945 Engels (B)
1946 Depredomme (B)
1947 Depoorter (B)
1948 Mollin (B)
1949 Danguillaume (F)
1950 Depredomme (B)
1951 Kubler (Sw)
1952 Kubler (Sw)
1953 de Hertog (B)
1954 Ernzer (L)
1955 Ockers(B)
1956 de Bruyne (B)
1957 Schoubben (B) & Derycke (B)
1958 de Bruyne (B)

1959	de Bruyne (B)	**1969**	Merckx (B)	**1979**	Thurau (WG)
1960	Geldermans (Nl)	**1970**	de Vlaeminck (B)	**1980**	Hinault (F)
1961	van Looy (B)	**1971**	Merckx (B)	**1981**	Fuchs (Sw)
1962	Planckaert, J. (B)	**1972**	Merckx (B)	**1982**	Contini (I)
1963	Melckenbeeck (B)	**1973**	Merckx (B)	**1983**	Rooks (Nl)
1964	Bocklandt (B)	**1974**	Pintens (B)	**1984**	Kelly (Ir)
1965	Preziosi (I)	**1975**	Merckx (B)	**1985**	Argentin (I)
1966	Anquetil (F)	**1976**	Bruyère (B)	**1986**	Argentin (I)
1967	Godefroot (B)	**1977**	Hinault (F)	**1987**	Argentin (I)
1968	van Sweevelt (B)	**1978**	Bruyère (B)	**1988**	van der Poel (Nl)

SPEED RECORD: Adrie van der Poel, 38.806 kph in 1988
MOST VICTORIES: Eddy Merckx, 5

Liège-Bastogne-Liège

Despite its name, the second of the Ardennes classics hasn't always started in Liège. Spa was used once, and it has finished in Verviers. Whatever the course, the profile is always the same. The outward leg to Bastogne is hilly. The first half of the return leg is hillier still, and the second half is brutally so. The hills are not Alpine and are rarely cobbled, but some of them go on for two miles while others rise one foot in every six. The other major feature is unpredictable weather. Temperatures approaching the 70s have been known, but more often there have been snowstorms.

The first edition was held in 1890, making it the oldest classic by one year. Pierre Chany lists results from 1890 but makes it clear that the race was then for amateurs. *Vélo* starts its list in 1894 when the first pro winner was Leon Houa, who won the amateur race in 1890. One more odd fact is that there have been only eight record speeds—Richard Depoorter's 37.679 mph in 1943 lasted until 1973.

Despite the intervention of Hermann Buse of Germany in 1930, the race remained generally a Belgian affair until Ferdi Kubler arrived on the scene to win in 1951. He won again in 1952, waiting nearly until the end, sprinting past three riders and all the lead cars in Liège itself, a sprint that he subsequently claimed had lasted three miles. He also won the Flèche Wallonne, and therefore the *Weekend Ardennais* title, both years.

The 1957 race, held well into May, caused the most discussion and had an almost unbelievable outcome. The Flèche Wallonne had taken place under blue skies. But overnight the temperature dropped, turning the rain to hail and snow, and reducing visibility to a few yards. The return from Bastogne was a nightmare and more than half the field retired, refusing to believe that the race could possibly get back to Liège. Fred de Bruyne and Raymond Impanis, two of Belgium's toughest, were as frozen as statues, incapable of removing their own gloves. The Belgian officials issued hot drinks at the next feed station, in Houffalize.

Steep climbs and unpredictable weather make Liège-Bastogne-Liège one of the more grueling classics. Here, Johan van der Velde and others brave cold and snow.

The race went on, Jef Lahaye and Brian Robinson breaking away with five in pursuit. At Cierreux a railroad crossing gate stopped the five. Belgian rules, unlike those elsewhere, required them to wait for the gate to open. In the murky afternoon and not knowing that a handful of journalists were warming themselves in the railway inn, the five climbed the gate. Lahaye and Robinson were caught and one of the five, Germain Derycke, was the first to finish.

But then came Frans Schoubben, who had broken no rules. Derycke was disqualified and Schoubben delared the winner. But Schoubben pointed out that he had not contested the result. Then it was Derycke's turn to be generous, suggesting the Schoubben be declared equal first, and so some sort of justice was done.

One of the five offenders had been Louison Bobet, who was subsequently dropped. Refusing to quit, he finished more than 13 minutes down. Asked why he struggled on, knowing that he had no hope of finishing among the prizes, he replied simply, "It's my job." Theo Mathy reports that when Bobet entered the dining room that evening, Antonin Magne ordered all present to stand, stating, "A great champion is here." There have been greater all-rounders than Bobet, but Magne was right—there has been no greater champion.

In 1966, another Frenchman did his reputation justice. That was the year the young Felice Gimondi won two successive classics by riding away from the field and the world was hailing him as Anquetil's successor. Like Rik van Steenbergen before him, Anquetil was a proud man. Although his record in the classics is unimpressive, that day in Belgium he was untouchable. He left the lead bunch with 30 miles to go and won by five minutes from a group which included Gimondi and the young Eddy Merckx.

Merckx won his first of five victories in 1969, the year of the Flandria debacle in the Flèche Wallonne. By the time of Liège-Bastogne-Liège, three days later, Merckx was ready. On the outward leg he showed no interest at all, save to keep himself towards the front. Coming to the final third, he briefed Victor van Schil—the best climber, after Merckx, in the Faema team. They attacked on the next hill and got away. Up every hill after that van Schil led Merckx; down the other side Merckx led van Schil. They reached the finish eight minutes clear.

Roger de Vlaeminck's turn came the following year, but it earned him no credit, since there was a mystery about the finish. Six riders reached the Rocourt track and disappeared together into the tunnel linking the approach road with the track. De Vlaeminck emerged onto the track first and won by seconds. What happened in the tunnel has never been officially told and Merckx made no official protest. It was odd that a close bunch of six riders at one end of the tunnel should be so widely separated at the other end and it was odd that Roger's brother Eric de Vlaeminck made no effort to reach the inside of the track first on the only occasion when he reached the finish of a classic with a chance of victory.

Nothing could stop Merckx for long, and the next three years belonged to him. In 1972 the fans saw a true Merckx recital. The race finished at Verviers, but if it had been on the moon, Merckx would probably have won.

After the turn and feed at Bastogne, every move had a Molteni rider in it. Tino Tabak started the first real break, taking Frans Mintjens, of Molteni, to a lead of 2:45. Five climbs followed before the race radio broadcast the inevitable news of a break by Merckx, with Wim Schepers and Herman van Springel. They met the two leaders at the foot of the Côte de Wanne. Next came the Stockeu, neither the steepest nor longest hill, but the one with the most abrupt start, coming immediately after a 90-degree turn. Merckx applied the pressure steadily on the uphill and the others dropped away, Schepers last of all. From there to Verviers nothing dramatic happened. Over four more climbs, Merckx increased his lead with no fuss at all, to reach the finish 2:40 up on Schepers and 4:35 on van Springel.

Three days later Merckx won the Flèche Wallonne in an 11-man sprint. He jumped his chain onto the wrong sprocket on the uphill finish and had the utmost difficulty holding off Poulidor, who had probably never won a sprint in his career.

It was very different in 1973. The finish was back on the Rocourt track north of Liège, which was approached from the south. There was a sizeable lead group heading for Liège, but Merckx still won, outsprinting Verbeeck by the narrowest of margins. Merckx took a record fifth win in 1975.

Liège-Bastogne-Liège confirmed the arrival of Merckx's successor in 1977. Hinault's solitary victory in Ghent-Wevelgem proved little, but it wasn't solitary for long. Towards Liège Hinault answered every attack by Merckx and de Vlaeminck. He jumped on André Dierickx's wheel when he broke away, dropped Freddy Maertens, and outsprinted Dierickx for the win.

Hinault struck again in 1980—a race reminiscent of the 1957 epic. Of 174 starters, only 21 made it back. From the opening kilometer the riders had to contend with falling snow. After an hour the entire countryside was white and within two hours 100 riders had quit. With 45 miles to go Rudy Pévenage was caught after a long and valiant escape. Hinault, just recovered from a puncture and chase, emerged first at the top of the Haute Levée climb. At the next summit, the Rosier, his lead was already 2:13 and it increased at every checkpoint. Past the statue to Stan Ockers on the final climb, down into Liège and out of the center to Rocourt, Hinault sped to a final winning margin of 9:24, bringing comparisons with Fausto Coppi into the minds of the older journalists.

By comparison the 1984 race showed the result of indecision. Laurent Fignon and Phil Anderson, watching each other like hawks after a late and apparently successful attack, failed to watch their backs adequately. A group of six caught them a mile from the finish and Sean Kelly won the sprint from Anderson and American Greg LeMond.

For the next three years the race belonged to Moreno Argentin. In 1985 he followed a successful break by Anderson and Stephen Roche to join Claude Criquielion in a four-man attack, from which he won the sprint. In 1986 it was a similar story with a four-man break and a winning sprint, and in 1987 there were five in the sprint. They may not have been great victories in the Merckx-Hinault mold, but it is a very rare rider who can win this race three successive years—Merckx was the only other to do so. The race was marred in 1988 by a major pileup after 60 miles that sent Fignon and American Davis Phinney to the hospital for stitches. The cause was a large drainage channel cut across the road that took the riders by surprise. The crash delayed 30 men, but a large group sped away shortly after in the fastest-ever Liège-Bastogne-Liège. Robert Millar attacked with 30 miles to go and was joined by Michel Dernies and Adrie van der Poel.

Phil Anderson (right) and Laurent Fignon had a break that seemed headed for success in the 1984 Liège-Bastogne-Liège. But the two were so busy watching each other that they neglected to watch behind them, and were caught by six others with a mile to go.

Steven Rooks stayed back to block for his teammate van der Poel, who outsprinted Dernies and Millar with relative ease. Rooks came in fourth, just ahead of Kelly and the main field.

From 1950–64, when the Ardennes classics were run on successive days, there was an official classification of the *Weekend Ardennais*, with a separate prize list. Points were awarded to the top finishers in the two races with, in the event of a tie, the higher placing in Liège-Bastogne-Liège being the determining factor. Here are the results, with my own calculations from 1965 onwards.

1950	Impanis (B)	**1963**	Poulidor (F)	**1976**	Maertens (B)
1951	Kubler (Sw)	**1964**	Bocklandt (B)	**1977**	de Vlaeminck (B)
1952	Kubler (Sw)	**1965**	Preziosi (I)	**1978**	Laurent (F)
1953	Storms (B)	**1966**	Dancelli (I)	**1979**	Hinault (F)
1954	Ernzer (L)	**1967**	Merckx (B)	**1980**	Hinault (F)
1955	Ockers (B)	**1968**	Godefroot (B)	**1981**	Mutter (Sw)
1956	van Genechten (B)	**1969**	Merckx (B)	**1982**	Kelly (I)
1957	Schoubben (B)	**1970**	de Vlaeminck (B)	**1983**	Bittinger (Sw)
1958	de Bruyne (B)	**1971**	Verbeeck (B)	**1984**	Anderson (A)
1959	Schoubben (B)	**1972**	Merckx (B)	**1985**	Argentin (I)
1960	Geldermans (Nl)	**1973**	Merckx (B)	**1986**	Criquielion (B)
1961	van Looy (B)	**1974**	Verbeeck (B)	**1987**	Criquielion (B)
1962	Wolfshohl (WG)	**1975**	Merckx (B)	**1988**	Rooks (Nl)

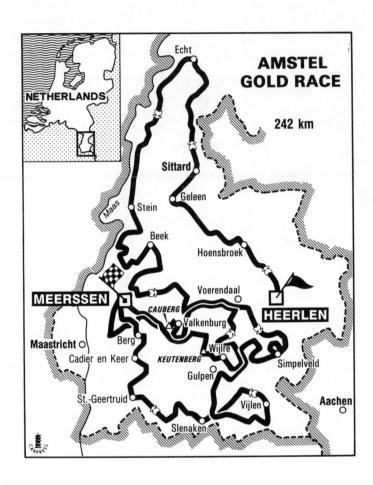

AMSTEL GOLD RACE

242 km

1966 Stablinski (F)	**1974** Knetemann (NI)	**1982** Raas (NI)
1967 Den Hartog (NI)	**1975** Merckx (B)	**1983** Anderson (A)
1968 Steevens (NI)	**1976** Maertens (B)	**1984** Hanegraaf (NI)
1969 Reybrouck (B)	**1977** Raas (NI)	**1985** Knetemann (NI)
1970 Pintens (B)	**1978** Raas (NI)	**1986** Rooks (NI)
1971 Verbeeck (B)	**1979** Raas (NI)	**1987** Zoetemelk (NI)
1972 Planckaert (B)	**1980** Raas (NI)	**1988** Nijdam (NI)
1973 Merckx (B)	**1981** Hinault (F)	

SPEED RECORD: Arie den Hartog, 43.711 kph in 1967
MOST VICTORIES: Jan Raas, 5

Amstel Gold Race

The Amstel Gold Race, newest of the classics, established itself very quickly on the international calendar. Though no race in the Netherlands could be called hilly, it is far from flat. The race is held in Limburg province where the hills, although shorter and less steep than those in the Ardennes, are liberally included. Moreover, the roads are often so narrow that it becomes a nightmare for journalists and team cars.

Unlike most classics, the Amstel is usually run on Saturday rather than Sunday. Like most classics, it has been won most often by home riders. This may seem surprising for a Dutch event, but Jan Raas won it in five of his nine professional seasons, doing a lot for the home statistics.

Raas is the central character in the story of the Amstel. A brilliant sprinter, he came close to becoming the only rider to win any classic five years running, but his performances showed other abilities as well as finishing speed.

His recital began in Valkenberg in 1977, scene of the world championship road race some years before. Bursting clear on a cart track that rose one foot in six, he was joined by compatriots Hennie Kuiper and Gerrie Knetemann. The Dutch trio performed heroics in their attempt to stay clear of a chasing group which included Walter Godefroot, Eddy Merckx, Freddy Maertens, Roger de Vlaeminck, Francesco Moser, Raymond Poulidor, and Herman van Springel. They did stay clear and Raas won a highly tactical sprint over his two teammates, suggesting that he could make a million on the track if he ever wanted to.

The next year Moser started the action on the Keuteberg, another cart track in Limburg, causing the lead bunch to split into three parts. Kuiper attacked from the front group in Valkenberg, with Raas on his wheel. Raas was away over the top and stayed away to finish, despite a chase that included Joop Zoetemelk, Moser, Kuiper, Maertens, and Knetemann. In 1979 it was a similar story, with Raas countering a late break and then taking off alone. The only difference was that the chasing group was of a far lesser quality, prompting one joker to suggest that the stars were sick of Raas. It could have been true.

1980 was different. Though Raas, reigning world champion, won, it indirectly cost him the chance of a quintuple record. Nine riders survived to contest the sprint in Meersen. Six of them tried desperately to get clear before the finish, fearing the Raas sprint, but every time they were brought back by Sean Kelly or Bernard Hinault, with Raas sitting on the appropriate wheel looking pleased with life. Hinault launched the sprint from way out, obviously to get himself clear of any tangle. Fons de Wolf came up and passed with Raas on his wheel. Then Raas switched slightly—not enough to be dangerous, not enough to earn disqualification, but just enough to cut Hinault's momentum—and the race was over. Raas again.

After the finish Hinault said that it was his last appearance in the Amstel, but he had overlooked one thing. The top echelon of professional riders are known as *hors categorie*, a level above first category. They are not allowed to race anywhere in the world on the day of a classic other than in the classic. So Hinault could choose either to stay away in 1981 or to swallow his pride and ride again.

After two long breaks by pairs of minor riders, the main field reassembled for the last 10 miles and approached the finish to sprint it out. Hinault went for a long sprint again, but this time there was a strong crosswind and Hinault noticed it. He took the right side of the road, where the spectators gave him the best shelter, and jumped hard. Raas got almost up to him, but saw no way inside. He pulled away, moved left into the wind,

Five-time winner Jan Raas (right) is the undisputed king of the Amstel Gold Race. Climbing the Cauberg in 1982 he keeps a eye on followers (from left) Jos Lammertink, Stephen Roche, and Sean Kelly.

and was lost, placing fourth, as Hinault stayed clear to take a sweet revenge.

Raas won again for the last time in 1982, but the final accolade goes to another of his compatriots, Joop Zoetemelk. World champion in 1985 at age 38, Zoetemelk had a disappointing 1986 and must have thought of retirement, but decided on one more year. Not for the first time, the Keuteberg forced the vital break and Zoetemelk was one of the 11 members. The Cauberg came next, and possibly bitter memories for Zoetemelk, who had broken away here in 1986 with Steven Rooks, only to be comfortably outsprinted. Rooks went with him again, taking along Malcom Elliott, an Englishman on a rare visit to the Continent. Zoetemelk must have dreaded the thought that history would repeat itself while Elliott, a sprinter of some note, must have hoped that he could just stay with the talented two. Just behind them was Leo van Vliet, already winner of two classics in 1987. When Zoetemelk moved smoothly away—at 40 Zoetemelk rarely jumped—the sprinters looked at each other and Rooks wondered what course of action to take. By then it was too late, for Zoetemelk once clear is rarely caught. His lead increased to half a minute at the finish where an almost delirious crowd realized that fairy tales occasionally do come true.

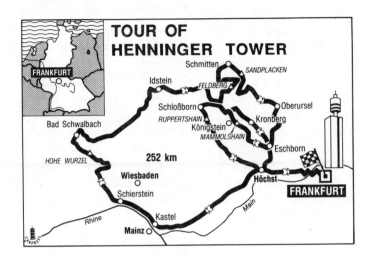

TOUR OF HENNINGER TOWER

FRANKFURT

Schmitten · SANDPLACKEN
Idstein
FELDBERG
Schloßborn · Oberursel
RUPPERTSHAIN · Kronberg
Bad Schwalbach · Königstein
MAMMOLSHAIN
Eschborn
HOHE WURZEL · **252 km**
Wiesbaden · Höchst
Schierstein · FRANKFURT
Rhine · Kastel · Main
Mainz

1962	Desmet, A. (B)	1971	Merckx (B)	1980	Baronchelli (I)
1963	Junkermann (WG)	1972	Bellonne (F)	1981	Jacobs (B)
1964	Roman (B)	1973	Pintens (B)	1982	Peeters, L. (B)
1965	Stablinski (F)	1974	Godefroot (B)	1983	Peeters, L. (B)
1966	Hoban (GB)	1975	Schuiten (Nl)	1984	Anderson (A)
1967	van Ryckeghem (B)	1976	Maertens (B)	1985	Anderson (A)
1968	Beugels (Nl)	1977	Knetemann (Nl)	1986	Wampers (B)
1969	Pintens (B)	1978	Braun (WG)	1987	Lauritzen (N)
1970	Altig (WG)	1979	Willems (B)	1988	Dernies (B)

SPEED RECORD: Gerrie Knetteman, 41.996 kph in 1977
MOST VICTORIES: Georges Pintens, Ludo Peeters, and Phil Anderson, 2 each

Tour of Henninger Tower (Frankfurt Grand Prix)

Although the Tour of Henninger Tower is one classic where home riders don't hold a majority of the victories, the advantage of riding on home roads is seen with three West German winners and several more who have come close. Also known as the Frankfurt Grand Prix, the race is held in the Taunus Mountains west of Frankfurt on a figure-eight course, with over 5,000 vertical feet of climbing, most of it gentle but adding up to a considerable test of stamina. Spectators with fast cars can see the race four times, since it reaches the Glashütten and Höchst crossroads twice each, before heading downhill into Frankfurt for three laps of a circuit to the finish.

The Tour of Henninger Tower did not get official classic status until 1967, when the cycling world governing body named it as a replacement for Paris-Brussels, which could no longer be held. Since the race of the two capitals was resumed, the Henninger Tour has retained its position as a race of such importance that first category pros are not allowed to compete elsewhere on the same day.

Nobody has won it three times and, oddly enough, Eddy Merckx won only once. For the first few years it tended to go to the fastest survivor of a small group. Merckx gave the race a new status by winning alone in 1971, but the following year saw an upset. Gilbert Bellonne, a French climber of some repute, broke away on the last major climb, helped by his German-backed team. The field let him go, expecting to pull him back on the descent into Frankfurt. But they waited too long and even Merckx in full cry was unable to reduce the deficit, placing second. The next year Georges Pintens set a record speed while outsprinting Jurgen Tschan of West Germany. Since then Dietrich Thurau and Rolf Gölz have also been narrowly beaten in front of their countrymen, Thurau twice.

There were no such hard luck stories in 1974, just one of the great sprint finishes. A lone winner is an impressive and meritorious sight, but the prospect of four of the top sprinters in the world battling it out with scrupulous fairness is something else. Freddy Maertens and Frans Verbeeck were on one side of the road, Merckx and Walter Godefroot on the other, all going hell for leather for the line, with Marc de Meyer, André Dierickx and Walter Planckaert just behind them. Two years later there was a similar story with 10 top Belgian road sprinters going for the line, Maertens being judged the winner.

The speed record was set by Gerrie Knetemann in 1977, but his was the only smile on the podium that day. A record crowd had turned out to see Thurau, the idol of West Germany since the retirement of Rudi Altig, but Thurau fell victim to the Raleigh team tactics. There's no question that he was the strong man of the race, and the crowds lining the route went wild on the two occasions when he escaped from the bunch. But he was reeled in both times and it was his misfortune that the next break happened to be by another Raleigh man. Knetemann was probably doing little more than testing the waters when he poked his nose in front with 20 miles to go, but

The Frankfurt fans cheer a jubilant Adrie van der Poel at the finish of the 1983 Henninger Tower race. Van der Poel wasn't so happy when he was later disqualified for doping, with the race going to Ludo Peeters.

there was no response from the bunch. He quickly shot into a lead of two minutes that he never appeared to be losing. In the last kilometer Thurau was allowed to make his successful bid for second, and it was Verbeeck's turn to look miserable. Third, second, second, third was Verbeeck's record—one that he clearly didn't want.

In the 1980s Ludo Peeters and Phil Anderson have been the dominant figures, but the most significant victory was Dag-Otto Lauritzen's in 1987, which gave Norway her first classic winner. The key break was started by the Wijnants brothers, Ludwig and Jan, riding for different teams. Six riders bridged the gap and the break was on, with Lauritzen and Bob Roll of the 7-Eleven team perhaps the most unlikely members. The break developed a lead of more than a minute. With no recognized sprinters up front, it seemed anybody's race despite the frantic efforts of Anderson, keen to take a third victory. Lauritzen, a major figure in the break, crossed the line first. Later that summer he confirmed his talent by a brilliant stage win in the Tour de France.

1935	Deloor, G. (B)	1959	Suarez (Sp)	1975	Tamames (Sp)
1936	Deloor, G. (B)	1960	de Mulder (B)	1976	Pessarodona (Sp)
1937–40	not held	1961	Soler (Sp)	1977	Maertens (B)
1941	Berrendero (Sp)	1962	Altig (WG)	1978	Hinault (F)
1942	Berrendero (Sp)	1963	Anquetil (F)	1979	Zoetemelk (Nl)
1943–44	not held	1964	Poulidor (F)	1980	Ruperez (Sp)
1945	Rodriguez, D. (Sp)	1965	Wolfshohl (WG)	1981	Battaglin (I)
1946	Langarica (Sp)	1966	Gabica (Sp)	1982	Lejarreta (Sp)
1947	van Dyck (B)	1967	Janssen (Nl)	1983	Hinault (F)
1948	Ruiz (Sp)	1968	Gimondi (I)	1984	Caritoux (F)
1950	Rodriguez, E. (Sp)	1969	Pingeon (F)	1985	Delgado (Sp)
1951–54	not held	1970	Ocana (Sp)	1986	Pino (Sp)
1955	Dotto (F)	1971	Bracke (B)	1987	Herrera (Co)
1956	Conterno (I)	1972	Fuente (Sp)	1988	Kelly (Ir)
1957	Lorono (Sp)	1973	Merckx (B)		
1958	Stablinski (F)	1974	Fuente (Sp)		

SPEED RECORD: Eric Caritoux, 39.869 kph in 1984
MOST VICTORIES: Gustave Deloor, J. Berrendero, José Fuente, and Bernard Hinault, 2 each

Tour of Spain (Vuelta d'España)

The Tour of Spain (*Vuelta d'España*), created in 1935, has a checkered history. Interrupted by the Spanish Civil War and resumed in 1941, it became firmly established only in the mid 1950s. In the early 1980s it was threatened again by lack of sponsorship and the disatisfaction of the cycling world governing body, the Union Cycliste Internationale, about some aspects of its promotion. But its main problem is scheduling. Held in late April and early May, it conflicts with from two to five classics, and can rarely guarantee a first-class field.

The Vuelta was originally a two-week race, but has been expanded to three weeks in recent years. The distance of the 1989 race is 3,665 kilometers (2,291 miles). As with most stage races the route is not the same each year. A typical Vuelta might start on the Mediterranean coast, head for the lower passes in the Pyrenees, then move westward to the Cantabrian mountains, which often play a crucial part in the race. After a few easy days in the south, the race may cross the Sierra de Guadarrama and finish in Madrid.

Never dominated but often won by Spaniards, the Vuelta has a peculiar mixture of winners. Many home riders' entire reputation rests on their one victory but a couple—Luis Ocana and José Fuente—were respected outside of Spain. France and Belgium provided minor winners and some great ones like Jacques Anquetil, Bernard Hinault, and Eddy Merckx. And Italians like Felice Gimondi and Giovanni Battaglin made rare sorties. One or two victors, like Freddy Maertens, have won by reputation rather than by outriding their rivals and at least a couple—Rudi Altig and Rolf Wolfshohl—allegedly stole the race.

If one year's race can be said to have brought international fame to the

The story of the 1962 Vuelta is one of team tactics—good and bad. Jacques Anquetil, heading the St. Raphael team, hoped for a victory that would make him the first to win all three major national tours. A week into the race his overall position was a little behind teammates Rudi Altig (right) and Seamus Elliott (left). But while Elliott faithfully served his captain, Altig rode his own race, beating Anquetil in a time trial and eventually winning overall.

Vuelta, it was 1962. Anquetil, lord of the peloton where stage races were concerned, had won the Tour de France twice, and was the first Frenchman to win the Giro. He came to Spain intent on becoming the first to win all three big national tours, bringing with him one of the finest St. Raphael teams ever assembled—they won 12 of the 16 stages.

After a week Anquetil was in a marvelous position, close to the lead held by Altig from Seamus Elliott. Since both were on his own team, Anquetil enjoyed an armchair ride while the Spanish teams attacked. Altig and Elliott had shared the lead, apparently happily, until stage nine, during which Altig punctured when the team car was unavailable. As leader, he expected to receive a wheel from a teammate, but none was offered. This put Elliott back into the lead at the end of the stage and left Altig furious.

Over the next five stages Elliott was in a winning break four times but refused to share the work out of loyalty to his captain. There is little doubt that he would have won, had he not been so unselfish. Anquetil was expected to assert himself during the time trial, but Altig won that stage and took over the leader's jersey. Anquetil went home in disgust and Elliott spent the rest of a race that he could have won defending Altig.

There were no mistakes the next year and Anquetil achieved his ambition of being the first rider to win the Vuelta, Giro, and Tour. Raymond Poulidor followed with a win in 1964 and was expected to take a second victory in 1965 but Wolfshohl, a teammate, thought otherwise and was right.

When a Spaniard won it was usually an ephemeral honor, but Ocana was different. Although his career was not richly studded with victories, he did go on from his Vuelta win to take the Tour de France in 1973. And in 1971 he caused one of the great upsets in the post-war history of that race when he massacred Merckx in the Alps.

Sandwiching Merckx's lone Vuelta win was a double by Fuente, another brilliant climber and, like Ocana, afraid of nobody. Although he never won a major race outside Spain, Fuente was often a challenge to Merckx in the Giro.

The farce came in 1977 with the entry of Maertens, reputedly the fastest road rider in the world. He had set his sights on winning the Giro and went to Spain for suitable training. As it happened he won a record 13 stages, the points title, and the race, but later crashed out of the Giro when only 16 seconds down on the leader. In the Vuelta, Maertens' very presence seemed to intimidate the domestic field. Supported through the mountains by his faithful lieutenant, Michel Pollentier (who won the Giro after Maertens' crash), he was hardly ever attacked.

The same could not be said of Hinault the following year. It seemed that every Spanish team had signed a pact to overthrow the invader, but with the help of teammate Jean-René Bernardeau, Hinault took the win by under three minutes. It wasn't ideal terrain for Hinault, since the high passes are not open at the time of the race. Moreover, the Frenchman's autocratic manner seemed to bring out the worst in the Spanish spectators.

For the first week of the 1981 Vuelta it looked as though Hinault would have a new rival in France, with Regis Clere sweeping all before him. But it virtually ended for Clere with a time trial in the Sierra Nevada that gained 4,000 feet. Clere finished ninth, and lost four minutes to Battaglin, who, climbing the slopes at an average speed of 16 mph, took the lead.

When Vincente Belda attacked him in the Pyrenees, Battaglin, as cool as he was gifted, calmly rode upward at his own speed while Belda gained three minutes and the race lead. Two miles from the summit, Battaglin counterattacked. He sprinted uphill and finished on a massive gear, reducing his deficit to well under a minute and confirming that nobody was going to take the race from him. Ten days later Battaglin started the Giro and became one of only two—Merckx was the other—to win the Vuelta and Giro in the same year.

It was another farce in 1982. Angel Arroyo was the apparent victor, climbing superbly on stage 15 to confirm his position and finishing third on a mountainous stage 17 behind Pedro Munoz and Belda. All was well until the dope test revealed proscribed substances in the urine samples of the first three. The sanctions moved Arroyo down to 16th, 8:05 behind Marino Lejarreta, who became the winner by default.

The following year Lejarreta came within 1:16 of a second victory, this time over Hinault. It was one of Hinault's least satisfactory wins, owed largely to help received officially from teammate Laurent Fignon and unofficially from Giuseppe Saronni whose main aim in riding was to prepare his bid for the Giro.

Hinault was followed in 1984 by another Frenchman, Eric Caritoux, whose ousting of Pedro Delgado in the Cantabrian Mountains brought out the worst in the Spanish spectators. Caritoux was abused, spat upon, and stoned during the days that followed. At times he had to be given a police escort and there were rumors of sabotage prior to the final time trial. Caritoux survived that, but lost time to Alberto Fernandez, who had closed to within six seconds with one day to go. The Spaniards tried everything, but couldn't shake off Caritoux on the roads to Madrid, and Caritoux won by six seconds, the smallest margin in the history of the three major stage races.

For the next two years Robert Millar dominated the Vuelta, but finished second both times. The British press found a whole range of excuses for Millar's defeats, but the truth is that winning depends upon many factors and Millar was deficient in two of them—he had a poor sense of tactics, and he lacked adequate team support.

Millar was in the lead in 1985 and in position to win when the race reached the Sierra de Guadarrama. With only two stages left Millar punctured, which was sheer misfortune but always likely to happen and not usually serious. It was also, predictably, the signal for a general Spanish attack. Less expected was the poor quality of service from his Peugeot team, not only in getting him back on the bike, but in feeding him news of an attack ahead, which included Delgado.

Delgado was sixth overall, six minutes behind Millar. But the Spanish teams combined to help him gain an unprecedented seven minutes and the win. It was subsequently argued that the Spanish break was given shelter behind team cars and other vehicles illicitly present, but there was no evidence. Where Millar failed was in not organizing the chase himself in the company of a number of strong riders who, as Sean Kelly later stated, would undoubtedly have helped him.

Millar had the race lead again the next year but lost it to Alvaro Pino, a rider far less to be feared than Delgado. It can't be said whether Pino, had he been attacked immediately, would have been able to resist. But Millar seemed to feel that there was plenty of time. Perhaps he was gambling on the final time trial to recover the half minute by which Pino led. Millar rode well but Pino was inspired and he won the time trial and the race.

There is an ironic footnote to Millar's two near wins. Nobody has been King of the Mountains in the national tours of France, Italy, and Spain. Millar has won the title in two, but not in the race he came closest to winning—the Tour of Spain.

The Vuelta of 1987 may prove the most significant for years to come.

A slight twitch or misjudgment can bring a rider—or a whole pack—down. Damage to bikes and gear is costly, but the real risk is torn muscles and broken bones.

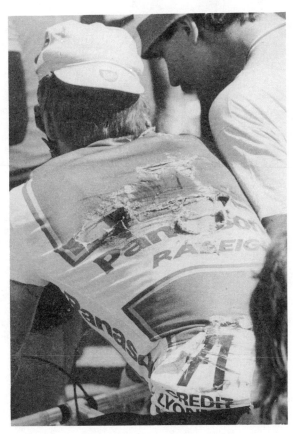

Colombians had won minor stage races, had looked good in the mountains for several seasons, but had never really seemed up to taking overall victory in a major stage race. Now that has changed and, despite their still generally disappointing performances, they know that they can win. It was Luis Herrera who took the honors with a total of eight Colombians in the top 20. Nearly all of the Colombian riders can climb, several are learning fast how to time trial, they have avoided being dropped on trivial stages through inattention, five have concentrated practice in stage race strategy, and who knows how many races they will be winning in the 1990s?

In the three major stage races there are secondary classifications as well as the main one based on time. Of these, the most important are the King of the Mountains prize, given to the rider with the best climbing record, and the points title, won by the rider with the most consistently high finishing positions. Here are the mountain and points winners in the Vuelta.

KING OF THE MOUNTAINS

1935	Molinar (I)	**1968**	Gabica (Sp)
1936	Molina (Sp)	**1969**	Ocana (Sp)
1941	Trueba (Sp)	**1970**	Tamames (Sp)
1942	Berrendero (Sp)	**1971**	Zoetemelk (Nl)
1945	Berrendero (Sp)	**1972**	Fuente (Sp)
1946	Rodriguez, E. (Sp)	**1973**	Abilleira (Sp)
1947	Rodriguez, E. (Sp)	**1974**	Abilleira (Sp)
1948	Ruiz (Sp)	**1975**	Oliva (Sp)
1950	Rodriguez (Sp)	**1976**	Oliva (Sp)
1955	Buratti (I)	**1977**	Torres (Sp)
1956	Defilippis (I)	**1978**	Oliva (Sp)
1957	Bahamontes (Sp)	**1979**	Yanez (Sp)
1958	Bahamontes (Sp)	**1980**	Fernandez (Sp)
1959	Suarez (Sp)	**1981**	Laguia (Sp)
1960	Karmany (Sp)	**1982**	Laguia (Sp)
1961	Karmany (Sp)	**1983**	Laguia (Sp)
1962	Karmany (Sp)	**1984**	Yanez (Sp)
1963	Jimenez (Sp)	**1985**	Laguia (Sp)
1964	Jimenez (Sp)	**1986**	Laguia (Sp)
1965	Jimenez (Sp)	**1987**	Herrera (Co)
1966	San Miguel (Sp)	**1988**	Pino (Sp)
1967	Diaz (Sp)		

POINTS WINNER

1955	Magni (I)	**1972**	Perurena (Sp)
1956	van Steenbergen (B)	**1973**	Merckx (B)
1957	Iturat (Sp)	**1974**	Perurena (Sp)
1958	Botella (Sp)	**1975**	Lasa (Sp)
1959	van Looy (B)	**1976**	Thurau (WG)
1960	de Cabooter (B)	**1977**	Maertens (B)
1961	Suarez (Sp)	**1978**	van den Haute (B)
1962	Altig (WG)	**1979**	de Wolf, A. (B)
1963	Maliepaard (Nl)	**1980**	Kelly (Ir)
1964	Perez-Frances (Sp)	**1981**	Cedena (Sp)
1965	van Looy (B)	**1982**	Mutter (Sw)
1966	van der Vleuten (B)	**1983**	Lejarreta (Sp)
1967	Janssen (Nl)	**1984**	van Calster (B)
1968	Janssen (Nl)	**1985**	Kelly (Ir)
1969	Steegmans (B)	**1986**	Kelly (Ir)
1970	Reybrouck (B)	**1987**	Gutierrez (Sp)
1971	Guimard (F)	**1988**	Kelly (Ir)

GIRO
1988

1909	Ganna (I)	1931	Camusso (I)	1954	Clerici (Sw)	1973	Merckx (B)
1910	Galetti (I)	1932	Pesenti (I)	1955	Magni (I)	1974	Merckx (B)
1911	Galetti (I)	1933	Binda (I)	1956	Gaul (L)	1975	Bertoglio (I)
1912	Atala (Team)	1934	Guerra (I)	1957	Nencini (I)	1976	Gimondi (I)
1913	Oriani (I)	1935	Bergamaschi (I)	1958	Baldini (I)	1977	Pollentier (B)
1914	Calzolari (I)	1936	Bartali (I)	1959	Gaul (L)	1978	de Muynck (B)
1915–18	not held	1937	Bartali (I)	1960	Anquetil (F)	1979	Saronni (I)
1919	Girardengo (I)	1938	Valetti (I)	1961	Pambianco (I)	1980	Hinault (F)
1920	Belloni (I)	1939	Valetti (I)	1962	Balmanion (I)	1981	Battaglin (I)
1921	Brunero (I)	1940	Coppi (I)	1963	Balmanion (I)	1982	Hinault (F)
1922	Brunero (I)	1941–45	not held	1964	Anquetil (F)	1983	Saronni (I)
1923	Girardengo (I)	1946	Bartali (I)	1965	Adorni (I)	1984	Moser (I)
1924	Enrici (I)	1947	Coppi (I)	1966	Motta (I)	1985	Hinault (F)
1925	Binda (I)	1948	Magni (I)	1967	Gimondi (I)	1986	Visentini (I)
1926	Brunero (I)	1949	Coppi (I)	1968	Merckx (B)	1987	Roche (Ir)
1927	Binda (I)	1950	Koblet (Sw)	1969	Gimondi (I)	1988	Hampsten (US)
1928	Binda (I)	1951	Magni (I)	1970	Merckx (B)		
1929	Binda (I)	1952	Coppi (I)	1971	Petterson (Sd)		
1930	Marchisio (I)	1953	Coppi (I)	1972	Merckx (B)		

SPEED RECORD: Roberto Visentini, 38.908 kph in 1986*
MOST VICTORIES: Alfredo Binda, Fausto Coppi, and Eddy Merckx, 5 each

* *Vélo* cites Giuseppe Saronni as the record holder at 38.900 kph in 1983. Over the race distance of 3,922 kilometers, this works out to 100:49:20, which was his exact riding time. Visentini's time was 100:48:02, which gives him the record, while Saronni won the race because of bonuses gained.

Tour of Italy
(Giro d'Italia)

In Italy the best rider is known as the *campionissimo* and the fans are deeply loyal to their native heroes. It is a land where outstanding riders often come in pairs. Much of the history of the Tour of Italy (*Giro d'Italia*) is colored by these facts.

The Giro was founded by Signori Costamagna, Cougnet, and Morgagni in 1909. The race normally lasts three weeks, starting the last week in May, and in 1989, will cover 3,586 kilometers (2,241 miles).

Italians dominated the Giro for 41 years. But don't think that the race was dull in that long period until Hugo Koblet became the first foreign winner in 1950. Far from it. The early years saw a number of experiments, such as victory determined by a points classification or victory to a team only with no individual classification. In 1914 the general classification according to the total time for each rider was finally established. That was the year Lauro Bordin made a solo break of 220 kilometers, a record believed to have lasted until Manuel Zeferino covered 330 kilometers alone in the Portugese race Oporto-Lisbon in 1984. (The current record is the 347-kilometer (217-mile) break of Loïc le Flohic in the 1986 edition of Bordeaux-Paris.)

Today Costante Girardengo, the first *campionissimo*, would probably be a superstar, but he lived too early, at a time when there were relatively few great races and when Italians were generally unwilling to travel widely to compete. In 1919 he won seven of the 10 stages of the Giro. In his 1923 victory he took eight stages, although his final margin was only a minute. Even he was eclipsed by Alfredo Binda, who won five times between 1925 and 1935. In the other six years Binda finished 2nd, 7th, and 16th, failed to finish twice, and in 1930, was paid not to ride, because the organizers feared that his presence would kill interest in the race. Less flamboyant perhaps than Girardengo, who marked his retirement in 1921 by dismounting from his bike and drawing a large cross in the dusty road, Binda was the complete roadman, the Italian equivalent of Henri Pélissier.

After Binda's final effort in 1935, when Vasco Bergamaschi—usually known as Singapore because of his Asiatic appearance—won, there was considerable speculation in Italy as to who would be the next champion. That year the King of the Mountains was young Gino Bartali, who went on to his first victory in 1936 and his second in 1937. Beaten the next two years, Bartali sought to reinforce his chances in 1940 by adding to his team the youngster who had just won the Tour of Piedmont. This was Fausto Coppi. Coppi won the Giro in 1940 and gave birth to the first great dual act of Italian cycling. He and Bartali were followed by Felice Gimondi and Gianni Motta, and Francesco Moser and Giuseppe Saronni.

How much Coppi would have won without the outbreak of World War II will remain a matter of speculation. He was able to continue racing until 1942, when he took the world hour record, but was then drafted into the desert war in Tunisia where he was captured in 1943.

Coppi's 21 stage victories in the Giro were only half Binda's amazing

A typical Giro course features many climbs in the Apennine mountains and the Alps, with dozens of hairpin turns and, not infrequently, snow and ice. The Rolli Pass, above, was one of four in the 21st stage of the 1986 race.

total of 42, but Coppi distinguished himself in the manner of his victory. The 1948 race was won by Fiorenzo Magni by 13 seconds when he and Ezio Cecchi were able to exploit the rivalry between Bartali and Coppi and steal first and second places. Magni was hissed and jeered by the crowd when he received his final pink jersey and Coppi swore revenge. It came the following year in a stage that has entered the legends of cycling.

The stage crossed the Alpine passes of Maddalena, Vars, Izoard, Montgenevre, and Sestrières. Coppi broke away alone before the summit of the Izoard pass and reached the finish line with more than 20 minutes on Bartali who was second. It was the end of Bartali as a serious rival.

Koblet's 1950 win brought the end of an era and the start of the modern period when riders from many countries have traveled to Italy to confront, and sometimes beat, the local heroes. The star of the 1950s was Charly Gaul, one of the finest climbers ever and a man who loved bad weather.

Pasquale Fornara led the 1956 Giro comfortably with Gaul in 11th when the route took the peloton over the Monte Bondone from Merano. What began as rain turned to snow and hail. Riders dropped by the dozen along the roughly surfaced mountain road, Fornara among them, but Gaul slogged on over the frozen mud to take his first major victory.

In 1957 Gaul made an unusual contribution to the result. Having shared first place with Louison Bobet for much of the race, Gaul was wearing the leader's pink jersey on the last flat stage before the Dolomites, where he was expected to confirm his success. During the stage Gaul felt the need to relieve an aching bladder, a situation by no means uncommon. Usually a rider slips quietly to the back of the pack, satisfies his need, and makes his way back to the front. The chances are he would not be attacked, since his rivals would know that it might be their turn next.

Scorning convention, Gaul dismounted in front of the bunch and threatened Bobet with an unexpected shower. Aided by Raphael Géminiani, Bobet responded by splitting the peloton in two. They and Gastone Nencini took the lead with Gaul trapped at the back, unable to bridge the gap. As the stage progressed, Géminiani punctured and was caught by Gaul. What Gaul promised to do to Géminiani was more appropriate to Gaul's former job as a butcher than a cyclist. Meanwhile, Nencini took the lead, knowing that Bobet could drop him in the mountains.

Over the final pass the next day Gaul, Bobet, Géminiani, Nencini, and Ercole Baldini were clear. Nencini had an inopportune puncture, at which time the French pair and Baldini jumped, with Gaul awaiting Nencini. Baldini refused to work, claiming that he could not help a Frenchman to dethrone a fellow Italian. Gaul towed Nencini back to the lead, which Nencini held to the end of the race.

Two years later Gaul again made headlines. With two days and five passes to go, Anquetil held the lead. At the foot of the last pass, Gaul jumped, sprinting uphill at a speed later estimated to be 18 mph, taking five minutes from Anquetil and becoming the first foreigner to win the Giro twice.

The 1960 Giro almost produced a most unlikely winner. Arnaldo Pambianco held the lead as the race approached the massive Stelvio Pass. The 9,048-foot Stelvio is the third highest pass in Europe and includes 48 hairpin bends. Before the pass Rik van Looy attacked. Van Looy was the foremost road sprinter in the world, but far too heavy to be a successful climber. Sadly, the sustained effort broke him and Pambianco reversed the gap by the end of the stage. Despite his failure, van Looy's effort was as courageous as any before or since.

A new rivalry in Italian cycling came in the 1960s, as Motta and Gimondi struggled for supremacy. Motta took the Giro in 1966, but his early promise faded quickly. Gimondi won three times. Then came Merckx, who won in 1968 but was disqualified in 1969 after a positive dope test, which was almost certainly the result of his being framed. If not for that setback, Merckx would probably have won the Giro seven times in a row. As it was, he returned in 1970 to prove his superiority, then withdrew for another year. Only when riding for the Italian Molteni team did Merckx make the race an annual fixture.

Sometimes the fans cheer and sometimes they jeer. Laurent Fignon, in the leader's pink jersey, is the subject of abuse from fans of Italian Francesco Moser during the fifth stage of the 1984 Giro. Moser won the stage and took over the lead, losing it to Fignon later in the race, but taking it back for good in the final time trial.

Bernard Hinault's is one of the best records. He entered and won three times, the first in 1980 with a brilliant break over the Stelvio in the company of his friend and teammate, Jean-René Bernardeau. Hinault took his second Giro in 1982 despite a concerted effort by all the Italian teams to unite against him and his third in 1985 despite Moser's time trialing ability.

In 1984 the race was dominated by Moser and Laurent Fignon. Fignon outrode the Italian in the mountains but the final grand test, again the Stelvio, was cancelled because the summit was allegedly covered with snow. There were those who claimed that aerial photographs had shown a clear road and that the stage had been changed to deny Fignon the opportunity to challenge Moser.

As it was, Fignon reached the final time trial 1:31 clear of Moser, holder of the world hour record. Knut Knudsen had recorded a stage-winning 51:50 on the same time trial course three years earlier. Fignon duplicated the achievement, but Moser rode a remarkable 49:26 to win the stage and the race he had dreamed of.

Moser thought that 1985 would bring a repeat performance as he started the time trial 1:15 down on Hinault, who was jeered and threatened by Italian fans. But Hinault lost only seven seconds and made his triple.

Another amazing race resulted in 1987 between the twin leaders of the Carrera team, Stephen Roche and 1986 winner Roberto Visentini. They had apparently agreed to let the race sort itself out until one of them had taken the overall lead, after which the other would ride as a loyal team member. For the first two weeks they worked amicably and the pair shared the lead until Visentini hammered Roche in a time trial to take a firm grip on the race—or so it seemed. Over the Forcetta di Monte Rest, 50 miles from the finish of stage 15, a lowly rider escaped. Robert Millar and Claudio Conti followed, Millar chasing mountain points, but Roche was unwilling to allow Millar any latitude. Eventually 12 riders got together, including all the contenders for final victory except Visentini. Roche was ordered to wait for him but refused. His personal mechanic was threatened with physical violence, but insisted on accompanying Roche. At the end of the stage Visentini was 7th overall, 3:12 behind Roche, who was promised instant dismissal from the team. This was nonsense, since no sponsor is likely to sack a man about to bring them millions of dollars worth of publicity. Visentini fell further and further behind, eventually retiring, as Roche went on to win. Was he disloyal to the original agreement? Almost certainly. What would have happened had he not encouraged the attack on Visentini? Robert Millar probably would have won.

Jean-François Bernard started the 1988 Giro brilliantly, but gave way to an unknown, Maximo Podenzana, who held the lead for nine days, after to a long break on the Adriatic coast. The mountains provided a change of direction and leadership as Andy Hampsten won at Selvino and Franco Chioccioli took the race lead. What happened two days later will become one of the great stories in the history of the Giro. On a brutal stage over the Gavia Pass in freezing conditions Erik Breukink and Hampsten saw all their major rivals drop well behind, some out of the race altogether. Breukink won the stage and Hampsten the pink jersey. Hampsten confirmed that he was entitled to the pink jersey four days later, winning a mountain time trial by 32 seconds over Visentini and more than a minute over Breukink. Hampsten survived an attack by Urs Zimmermann and a rain-slickened road in the final time trial to become the first American to win the Giro.

KING OF THE MOUNTAINS

1933	Binda (I)	**1964**	Bitossi (I)
1934	Bertoni (I)	**1965**	Bitossi (I)
1935	Bartali (I)	**1966**	Bitossi (I)
1936	Bartali (I)	**1967**	Gonzales (Sp)
1937	Bartali (I)	**1968**	Merckx (B)
1938	Valetti (I)	**1969**	Michelotto (I)
1939	Bartali (I)	**1970**	van den Bossche (B)
1940	Bartali (I)	**1971**	Fuente (Sp)
1946	Bartali (I)	**1972**	Fuente (Sp)
1947	Bartali (I)	**1973**	Fuente (Sp)
1948	Coppi (I)	**1974**	Fuente (Sp)
1949	Coppi (I)	**1975**	Oliva (Sp)
1950	Koblet (Sw)	**1976**	Oliva (Sp)
1951	Bobet (F)	**1977**	Fernandez (Sp)
1952	Géminiani (F)	**1978**	Suter (Sw)
1953	Fornara (I)	**1979**	Bortolotto (I)
1954	Coppi (I)	**1980**	Bortolotto (I)
1955	Nencini (I)	**1981**	Bortolotto (I)
1956	no award	**1982**	van Impe (B)
1957	Géminiani (F)	**1983**	van Impe (B)
1958	Brankart (B)	**1984**	Fignon (F)
1959	Gaul (L)	**1985**	Navarro (Sp)
1960	van Looy (B)	**1986**	Munoz (Sp)
1961	Taccone (I)	**1987**	Millar (GB)
1962	Soler (Sp)	**1988**	Hampsten (US)
1963	Taccone (I)		

In 1956, instead of having an overall mountains title, the organizers included three separate climbing competitions: Apennines (Bahamontes), Dolomites (Gaul), and Stelvio (del Rio). If not for this, it is likely that Bahamontes would have been King of the Mountains, and become the only rider to take the title in all three major national stage races.

POINTS WINNER

1966	Motta (I)	**1978**	Moser (I)
1967	Zandegu (I)	**1979**	Saronni (I)
1968	Merckx (B)	**1980**	Saronni (I)
1969	Bitossi (I)	**1981**	Saronni (I)
1970	Bitossi (I)	**1982**	Moser (I)
1971	Basso (I)	**1983**	Saronni (I)
1972	de Vlaeminck (B)	**1984**	Freuler (Sw)
1973	Merckx (B)	**1985**	van der Velde (Nl)
1974	de Vlaeminck (B)	**1986**	Bontempi (I)
1975	de Vlaeminck (B)	**1987**	van der Velde (Nl)
1976	Moser (I)	**1988**	van der Velde (Nl)
1977	Moser (I)		

1891	Mills (GB)	**1924**	Pélissier, F. (F)	**1959**	Bobet (F)
1892	Stéphane (F)	**1925**	Suter (Sw)	**1960**	Janssens (B)
1893	Cottereau (F)	**1926**	Benoit (B)	**1961**	van Est (Nl)
1894	Lesna (F)	**1927**	Ronsse (B)	**1962**	de Roo (Nl)
1895	Meyer (D)	**1928**	Martin (B)	**1963**	Simpson (GB)
1896*	Linton (GB) & Rivierre (F)	**1929**	Ronsse (B)	**1964**	Nedelec (F)
1897	Rivierre (F)	**1930**	Ronsse (B)	**1965**	Anquetil (F)
1898	Rivierre (F)	**1931**	van Rysselberghe (B)	**1966**	Janssen (Nl)
1899	Huret (F)	**1932**	Giyssels (B)	**1967**	van Coningsloo (B)
1900	Fischer, J. (G)	**1933**	Mithouard (F)	**1968**	Bodart (B)
1901	Lesna (F)	**1934**	Noret (F)	**1969**	Godefroot (B)
1902*	Wattelier (F) & Garin (F)	**1935**	de Caluwe (B)	**1970**	van Springel (B)
1903	Aucouturier (F)	**1936**	Chocque (F)	**1971–72**	not held
1904	Augereau (F)	**1937**	Somers (B)	**1973**	Mattioda (F)
1905	Aucouturier (F)	**1938**	Laurent (F)	**1974***	van Springel (B)
1906	Cadolle (F)	**1939**	Laurent (F)		& Délépine (F)
1907	van Hauwaert (B)	**1940–45**	not held	**1975**	van Springel (B)
1908	Trousselier (F)	**1946**	Masson, E. Jr. (B)	**1976**	Godefroot (B)
1909	van Hauwaert (B)	**1947**	Somers (B)	**1977**	van Springel (B)
1910	Georget (F)	**1948**	le Strat (F)	**1978**	van Springel (B)
1911	Faber (L)	**1949**	Moujica (F)	**1979**	Chalmel (F)
1912	Georget (F)	**1950**	van Est (Nl)	**1980**	van Springel (B)
1913	Mottiat (B)	**1951**	Gauthier (F)	**1981**	van Springel (B)
1914	Deman (B)	**1952**	van Est (Nl)	**1982**	Tinazzi (F)
1915–18	not held	**1953**	Kubler (Sw)	**1983**	Duclos-Lasalle (F)
1919	Pélissier, H. (F)	**1954**	Gauthier (F)	**1984**	Linard (F)
1920	Christophe (F)	**1955**	not held	**1985**	Martens (B)
1921	Christophe (F)	**1956**	Gauthier (F)	**1986**	Glaus (Sw)
1922	Pélissier, F. (F)	**1957**	Gauthier (F)	**1987**	Vallet (F)
1923	Masson, E. Sr. (B)	**1958**	Cieleska (F)	**1988**	Rault (F)

SPEED RECORD: André Chalmel, 47.061 kph in 1979
MOST VICTORIES: Hermann van Springel, 7

* In 1896 Linton won, but over the wrong route, and Rivierre, who placed second, shared the race. In 1902 there were two separate races held on different days. In 1974 van Springel was misdirected and took the wrong route. Délépine, who placed second, protested and was awarded an equal first.

Bordeaux-Paris

Bordeaux-Paris is the one classic still held during the season of national tours. Sometimes known as the *Derby de la Route* it has been held as a professional classic for longer than any other race. Its date has varied considerably as has its structure, but the present scheduling near the end of May, clashing with the Giro, seems to have found favor, and the new formula introduced in 1986 was an instant success.

Originally, pacing by bicycle was allowed, though cars were used from 1897–99. Motorcycle pacing began in 1930, then in 1933 mopeds took over. In 1986 pacing was scrapped completely and the race declared open to professionals and amateurs.

Because of this diversity of pacing methods several different speed records can be claimed, but André Chalmel's 1979 win was the fastest of all, at 47.061 kph. Further complications arise because, over the years, pacing was picked up at different points along the route—at the start, Poîtiers, Châtellerault, Sainte-Maure, Tours, Blois and Orléans. Chalmel collected his pacer in Poîtiers, the furthest point other than Bordeaux itself from the finish, but his record is still the one worth recording.

Vélo omits the 1891 race from its results since it was officially amateur. The distinction is blurred by the fact that the winner by more than an hour, George Mills, was paid 1,000 British pounds a year by Raleigh Cycles. Mills was officially a draftsman but continued to enter races as well as design bicycles and components.

For the first Bordeaux-Paris, camp beds were erected in the streets of Angoulême and many towns set up first-aid posts. It was anticipated that the race would take between three and four days. Mills ignored all this, winning in 26 ½ hours and firmly establishing the event.

In 1904 the first four riders were disqualified for strewing tacks behind them on the road. 1908 was even more unusual. Cyrille van Hauwaert and Louis Trousselier, riding well together and sharing the pace, held a four-

The Pélissier brothers, Francis (left) and Henri, were among the more successful and well-known riders of the early 20th century. They are shown here at the starting control of the 1922 Bordeaux-Paris, which Francis won. Henri took the race in 1919 and Francis had a second win in 1924.

minute lead. Then van Hauwaert needed to answer the call of nature. Trousselier agreed to wait but fixed a time limit, lest the chasers should catch them. After the agreed time had passed van Hauwaert was still behind a bush and Trousselier carried on alone to victory.

In 1930 Francis Pélissier came out of retirement in hopes of winning the special prize offered to the rider with the fastest finishing lap on the Paris track where the race ended. His brother and manager Henri had a bright idea. Instead of changing to a track bike at the velodrome entrance, which was then the custom, they would make the change at the top of the last hill to save time. All went well. Pélissier was riding to the finish with Georges Ronsse. After changing bikes, Pélissier caught Ronsse before the track and was a certain winner until disaster struck. An eager track official, unaware that Pélissier had already switched bikes, rushed to help him dismount, grabbing his saddle and sticking to him as Ronsse sprinted off to win.

In 1937 Joseph Somers won after collapsing in midrace and appearing delirious. He recovered and caught Louis Thiétard who then collapsed, leaving Somers to win. Somers repeated the feat 10 years later after the leader, Urbain Caffi, zigzagged over the top of a hill and fell off his bike almost unconscious.

During the 1950s Wim van Est and Bernard Gauthier dominated the race, but their battle was not the highlight of the decade. That belonged to

Louison Bobet, riding in 1959 against the orders of his doctor, and winning by attacking. Bobet had sworn to take the Derby before retiring and there were few dry eyes in France when he won.

One of the greatest Bordeaux-Paris victories of all was Jacques Anquetil's in 1965. As described in Anquetil's biography, Raphael Géminiani, his manager, had persuaded Anquetil that he could realistically attempt a double win of the Dauphiné Libéré and Bordeaux-Paris, even though the first race ended at 5 p.m. on a Saturday in Avignon and the second began seven hours later in Bordeaux, 350 miles away.

Arrangements were made to fly Anquetil from Avignon to Bordeaux and the entries to both races were confirmed. During the Dauphiné there was one terrible stage when Anquetil and Raymond Poulidor, coming over the top of the Chamrousse climb in thick fog, six minutes down on their rivals, refused the capes offered to them. They arrived, frozen, at the finish, but Anquetil's amazing constitution allowed him to withstand that stage and go on to win the race. The timetable was then:

4:58—finish of the last stage in Avignon
5:00—Anquetil on the podium as winner
5:10—a dash through the crowd to find his car and chauffeur
5:15—the car leaves the official parking lot
5:20—Anquetil reaches a hotel and has a bath
5:55—a high-speed car ride through villages to Nimes airport
6:30—into the airport for interviews
6:58—take-off

The other riders in Bordeaux-Paris had been ready and training for several days. Anquetil managed one hour's sleep in a Bordeaux hotel before the midnight start. In the early morning hours Anquetil's race seemed over. Frozen, soaked by the persistent rain, and with pains in his back he dismounted and changed into dry clothes. Photographers and reporters gathered round as the final moment seemed near. But Anquetil remounted and rode off into a headwind. Eight hours later Anquetil, Tom Simpson, and Jean Stablinski caught and dropped François Mahé who had been away for a long time. From that moment there could be only one outcome, as Simpson struggled to hold two riders from the same team. It was finally Anquetil who broke away to win alone by less than a minute. He never entered Bordeaux-Paris again.

In the early years Bordeaux-Paris twice had two winners, both for valid reasons. What happened in 1974 was shameful. Herman van Springel attacked in Tours, quickly establishing a lead that grew to 12:45. At a vital

Pacing was featured in Bordeaux-Paris from its inception until 1986. Seven-time winner Herman van Springel follows his pacer in the 1974 event, in which he was misdirected over the wrong route.
Nevertheless, van Springel was first over the line, but the second place rider protested, and they were both declared winners.

junction the police outrider pointed van Springel in the wrong direction. Van Springel took the wrong road with the race director following in his car, oblivious of the error. Two miles had been covered when the mistake was realized. The director instructed van Springel to take a new route, just over a mile longer than the original, which would bring him back to the correct route in another 12 miles. By the time van Springel returned to the course, his lead had been cut to 7:04. In no way discouraged, he resumed his effort and finished 14:25 ahead of Régis Délépine, who promptly claimed victory. The matter was eventually resolved by naming both as winners.

The next year van Springel won again, over the correct route, with Délépine again second. From 1970–81 van Springel won seven times. Twice he lost because of mishaps suffered while leading and twice the race was cancelled. Only once was he genuinely beaten. Had the race been held every year and van Springel been no more than ordinarily unlucky, he might have won it nine times or more. It must be said that van Springel's domination did nothing for the success of Bordeaux-Paris. Few riders were prepared to challenge him, to such an extent that one of his victories was over five other finishers from a field of only 10 starters.

In 1986 the organizers tried to revitalize the event. They abandoned pacing and invited amateurs and women to enter. The result was a start list of 139 with 56 finishing within the official time limit. After a marathon break by Loïc le Floic, a small group came together, but was whittled down to three for the final sprint, won by Gilbert Glaus. In 1987 there were 258 starters and 60 official finishers.

It may not be the Derby, but Bordeaux-Paris is certainly back on.

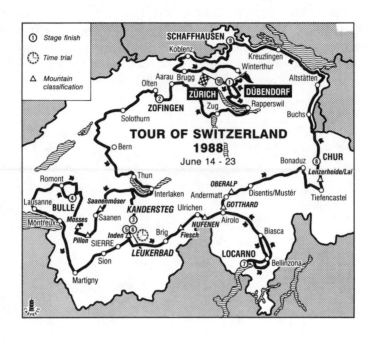

Tour of Switzerland 1988 — June 14-23 route map

Legend:
- ① Stage finish
- 🕐 Time trial
- △ Mountain classification

1933 Bulla (Au)	**1953** Koblet (Sw)	**1971** Pintens (B)
1934 Geyer (D)	**1954** Fornara (Sw)	**1972** Pfenninger (Sw)
1935 Rinaldi (F)	**1955** Koblet (Sw)	**1973** Fuente (Sp)
1936 Garnier (B)	**1956** Graf (Sw)	**1974** Merckx (B)
1937 Litschi (Sw)	**1957** Fornara (Sw)	**1975** de Vlaeminck (B)
1938 Valetti (I)	**1958** Fornara (Sw)	**1976** Kuiper (Nl)
1939 Zimmermann, R. (Sw)	**1959** Junkermann (WG)	**1977** Pollentier (B)
1940 not held	**1960** Ruegg (Sw)	**1978** Wellens (B)
1941 Wagner (Sw)	**1961** Moresi (I)	**1979** Wesemael (B)
1942 Kubler (Sw)	**1962** Junkermann (WG)	**1980** Beccia (I)
1943–45 not held	**1963** Fezzardi (I)	**1981** Breu (Sw)
1946 Bartali (I)	**1964** Maurer (Sw)	**1982** Saronni (I)
1947 Bartali (I)	**1965** Bitossi (I)	**1983** Kelly (Ir)
1948 Kubler (Sw)	**1966** Portalupi (Sw)	**1984** Zimmermann, U. (Sw)
1949 Weilenmann (Sw)	**1967** Motta (I)	**1985** Anderson (A)
1950 Koblet (Sw)	**1968** Pfenninger (Sw)	**1986** Hampsten (US)
1951 Kubler (Sw)	**1969** Adorni (I)	**1987** Hampsten (US)
1952 Fornara (I)	**1970** Poggiali (I)	**1988** Wechselberger (Au)

SPEED RECORD: Phil Anderson, 39.44 kph in 1985
MOST VICTORIES: Pasquale Fornara, 4

Tour of Switzerland

Although rarely considered a top stage race and often used nowadays as training for the Tour de France, Switzerland's national tour is a fine event, well off in terms of prize money and primes, and has a handsome pedigree. Lasting 10 days, the race usually crosses major Alpine passes twice, once each way. It boasts an imposing list of international winners, but has also known tragedy.

In 1948 the fourth stage led from Thun to Altdorf, via the Süsten Pass. The descent was on a broad, well-surfaced road with a long, curving tunnel. At the top Richard Depoorter had been dropped by a few seconds from a lead group of Jean Robic, Ferdi Kubler, and Stan Ockers. The story was told to me in a letter from René Jacobs.

"Depoorter had undertaken a high-speed pursuit of the leaders," Jacobs wrote. "It was said that he was traveling around 50 mph when he entered the tunnel, the furthest end of which could not be seen. In the darkness he hit the rock wall and rebounded into the middle of the road, where he was run over and killed by a following car. The car belonged to the Belgian delegation to the race and was driven by a certain Louis Hanssens. Also on board were Jean Leulliot (founder of Paris-Nice) and Guillaume Driessens (later a famous manager).

"I arrived on the scene a few minutes later and Francis Pélissier (then a manager) pointed out to me the tire marks on the chest of Depoorter's jersey. The driver of the car in question never admitted to hitting Depoorter, and the passengers reported neither feeling any shock nor noticing anything unusual. But a few days later, Leulliot sold to *Les Sports* (a Brussels newspaper) documents in which he confirmed that Depoorter had been run over. There was a court case in Brussels, in which I was called as a witness to what I had observed after the accident. Finally, Louis Hanssens was fined more than a million Belgian francs. Driessens, who fainted in court, continued to affirm that he knew nothing. The autopsy concluded that the cause of death was the crushing of the thoracic cage."

73

Picture-postcard villages make a spectacular setting for the Tour of Switzerland.

There have been many happier moments during the long history of this tour. Italian cyclists have regularly been among its stars, and Belgians were successful in 1970s, when Roger de Vlaeminck proved that he could survive the mountains to win a stage race. After eight years of victories by foreigners, Béat Breu's 1981 win brought a reawakening of Swiss pride, but the Swiss have not returned to dominate in the race.

Oscar Egg and Henri Suter in the 1920s, Ferdi Kubler and Hugo Koblet in the 1950s were among those who gave Switzerland a fine record for such a small country. Then came a long spell in the doldrums, with occasional flashes from the likes of Rolf Graf and Freddy Ruegg, an occasional track rider turning to the road like Louis Pfenniger (not to be confused with Fritz), and little else.

The arrival of Breu in the early 1980s sparked new interest in Switzerland in cycling. Older riders who hadn't been achieving much suddenly found a new zip, like Josef Fuchs with a win in Liège-Bastogne-Liège. In the 1981 Giro, 10 of the Swiss Cilo-Aufina team finished, with riders taking places among the top 5 in 11 stages. Although easily the finest Swiss team since the mid 1950s, most of the promise has since faded. One Swiss member, Daniel Gisiger, has twice won the Grand Prix of Nations, but lately the Swiss have been surpassed in their national tour by competitors from nations new to world cycling, such as Colombia and the United States.

Not since 1957–58 had any rider won the Swiss tour in successive years until Andy Hampsten burst upon the scene in 1986. Taking the prologue by surprise from Greg LeMond and Nikki Rüttimann, Hampsten lost his lead to Jean-Claude Leclercq in the stage-five time trial. He regained it the next day when he was one of seven who took 6:52 from Stefan Joho and 11:15 from Bernard Hinault. Despite a challenge from Robert Millar, Hampsten kept his lead to the end.

In 1987 Hampsten won by one second. The race had a series of leaders and it was not until the penultimate stage that Hampsten took over. Placing seventh, seven seconds behind Peter Winnen that day, Hampsten had only to hold off Winnen for the victory. He did, with fine team support from Roy Knickman and Jeff Pierce. Hampsten is the most likely transatlantic rider to ascend to LeMond's former status in the European peloton. But more important, Hampsten spearheads a 7-Eleven team which vies with Café de Colombia for the title of most exciting new team in pro cycling.

1903	Garin (F)				
1904	Cornet (F)				
1905	Trousselier (F)				
1906	Pottier (F)				
1907	Petit-Breton (F)				
1908	Petit-Breton (F)				

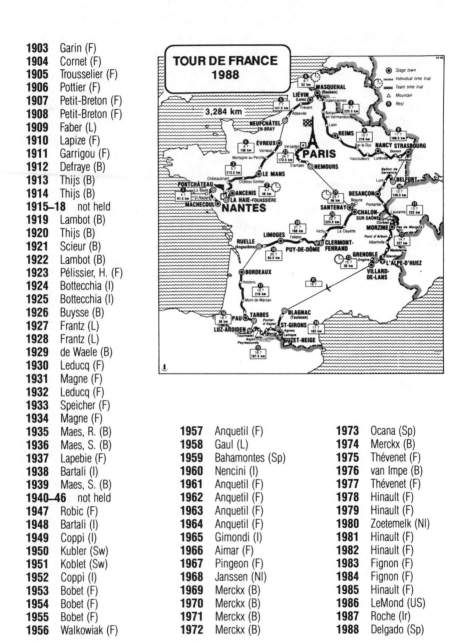

TOUR DE FRANCE
1988

3,284 km

- Stage town
- Individual time trial
- Team time trial
- Mountain
- Rest

1903 Garin (F)
1904 Cornet (F)
1905 Trousselier (F)
1906 Pottier (F)
1907 Petit-Breton (F)
1908 Petit-Breton (F)
1909 Faber (L)
1910 Lapize (F)
1911 Garrigou (F)
1912 Defraye (B)
1913 Thijs (B)
1914 Thijs (B)
1915–18 not held
1919 Lambot (B)
1920 Thijs (B)
1921 Scieur (B)
1922 Lambot (B)
1923 Pélissier, H. (F)
1924 Bottecchia (I)
1925 Bottecchia (I)
1926 Buysse (B)
1927 Frantz (L)
1928 Frantz (L)
1929 de Waele (B)
1930 Leducq (F)
1931 Magne (F)
1932 Leducq (F)
1933 Speicher (F)
1934 Magne (F)
1935 Maes, R. (B)
1936 Maes, S. (B)
1937 Lapebie (F)
1938 Bartali (I)
1939 Maes, S. (B)
1940–46 not held
1947 Robic (F)
1948 Bartali (I)
1949 Coppi (I)
1950 Kubler (Sw)
1951 Koblet (Sw)
1952 Coppi (I)
1953 Bobet (F)
1954 Bobet (F)
1955 Bobet (F)
1956 Walkowiak (F)

1957 Anquetil (F)
1958 Gaul (L)
1959 Bahamontes (Sp)
1960 Nencini (I)
1961 Anquetil (F)
1962 Anquetil (F)
1963 Anquetil (F)
1964 Anquetil (F)
1965 Gimondi (I)
1966 Aimar (F)
1967 Pingeon (F)
1968 Janssen (NI)
1969 Merckx (B)
1970 Merckx (B)
1971 Merckx (B)
1972 Merckx (B)

1973 Ocana (Sp)
1974 Merckx (B)
1975 Thévenet (F)
1976 van Impe (B)
1977 Thévenet (F)
1978 Hinault (F)
1979 Hinault (F)
1980 Zoetemelk (NI)
1981 Hinault (F)
1982 Hinault (F)
1983 Fignon (F)
1984 Fignon (F)
1985 Hinault (F)
1986 LeMond (US)
1987 Roche (Ir)
1988 Delgado (Sp)

SPEED RECORD: Pedro Delgado, 38.909 kph in 1988
MOST VICTORIES: Jacques Anquetil, Eddy Merckx, and Bernard Hinault, 5 each

Tour de France

Most enthusiasts would agree that the Tour de France is the world's greatest bicycle race. Some, myself included, would claim that it is the world's greatest sports spectacle. The Tour is a three-week race that in recent years has been held the first three weeks of July. The 1989 race will be one of the shortest ever, at 2,934 kilometers (1,834 miles). There may be occasional classics during the Vuelta and the Giro, but the Tour has no such competition. As well as demanding the greatest combination of talents in its individual winner, it often brings to the fore the qualities needed in a successful team.

Despite its status, it does have problems. The Union Cycliste Internationale has limited the overall length of the race and of individual stages. Messieurs Jacques Goddet and Felix Levitan, for so long the promoters uniquely connected with the Tour, enjoyed experimentation. It is largely because of them that the modern event has so many transfers—occasions when the finish of one stage and the start of the next are different places, sometimes a considerable distance apart. They have increased the use of mountain resorts for stage finishes, instead of such traditional towns as Briançon and Luchon, so that the field rides up a long cul-de-sac to finish at the very top. They began a strategy of interspersing courses entirely within France with an occasional start abroad, such as Berlin in 1987 and maybe Montreal in 1992. And they were responsible for that most unfair of innovations, the team time trial—and a glance at the 1987 race will show the unfairness.

The Tour is unique, as was its origin. In the late 1890s, the Dreyfus affair—a national scandal—divided France. The editor of *L'Auto* sought ways to counter circulation gains made by *Vélo*, a pro-Dreyfus paper. He called on Henri Desgrange, holder of the world hour record, for advice. Desgrange helped the paper promote its own version of Bordeaux-Paris in 1902, to compete with the original, which *Vélo* had sponsored since 1891.

As pro-Dreyfus sentiment swelled in the early 1900s, stronger measures were required to counter the new-found popularity of *Vélo*. Desgrange and his colleagues came up with the idea of a six-day race on roads: the Tour de France.

The route of the first Tour, in 1903, was:

Paris-Lyon	290 miles
Lyon-Marseille	230 miles
Marseille-Toulouse	270 miles
Toulouse-Bordeaux	170 miles
Bordeaux-Nantes	265 miles
Nantes-Ville d'Avray	290 miles.

The riders were allowed to quit one stage but still start the next. Doing this removed them from the general classification but they could continue to compete for stage prizes. Eventually Maurice Garin emerged as the winner. He had the fastest time in 1904 also, when the first four were disqualified for cheating.

In 1907 came Lucien Petit-Breton, setting a speed record of more than 15 mph which stood until 1931. He won again in 1908. The next Tour went to François Faber, who won six of the 11 stages and was always in the top 10. Desgrange decided to toughen the race by including the Pyrenees.

Hundreds of thousands of fans line the Champs Élysées for the finish of the Tour de France.

In 1913, five were leading the way over the Pyrenean passes when Eugène Christophe broke away on the unpaved Tourmalet, picking up five minutes. From the summit, he looked like a cloud of dust moving down the side of the mountain. Suddenly the cloud stopped. Christophe had fallen. He was unhurt, but his bike had a broken fork. In those days riders had to make their own repairs. Christophe shouldered his bike and ran down to a village. He found the smithy, lit the forge, worked the bellows, and repaired his broken fork. Philippe Thijs won the stage and the race, but because of this episode Christophe's name lives on in the hearts of Frenchmen.

Unlike Octave Lapize, Petit-Breton, and Faber, Christophe survived the war and was at the start in 1919. That year Desgrange introduced the yellow jersey, probably his most brilliant idea of all. After the Nice to Grenoble stage it was presented for the first time, to none other than Christophe. It was a stormy race. Henri Pélissier was cautioned for dangerous riding and quit the race the same evening, declaring that he would not tolerate being treated like a convict. In his statement, he coined the now famous description of professional cyclists—*les forçats de la route*—convicts of the road.

Christophe clung tenaciously to his jersey until the 295-mile stage from Metz to Dunkirk. With a third of the distance left he fell and once more broke his fork. Again he found a blacksmith's shop and repaired the damage. And again the stage winner won the race. This time it was Firmin Lambot, and he beat Christophe by three hours at the finish of the race.

Pélissier's victory came in 1923 when he introduced the method later copied so brilliantly by Jacques Anquetil. This was to stay near the front throughout, select a stage when he thought he would do well, take the lead, and sit on it. Pélissier chose the Izoard stage, attacked before the climb to gain a one-minute lead, extended it to six at the summit, and was never seriously challenged after. The next year he withdrew again, this time when a commissaire ordered him to remove his jersey and wear one that had official approval.

Another French hero was René Vietto, the perfect team rider. After a poor start in 1934 Vietto found the mountains to his liking and was improving so quickly that many pundits picked him to win. On the Hospitalet Pass his team captain Antonin Magne fell and broke a wheel. Vietto immediately handed over one of his and waited five minutes for the repair truck. The next day Magne broke another and called to Vietto, just ahead. Vietto rode back, handed over his wheel, and wept as he awaited the repair truck.

Compare Vietto's attitude with those of Anquetil and Roger Rivière who rode desperately to deny one another victory in 1959 and united only to

It isn't clear whether this cyclist is being caught or shoved, but rider interference can often affect the outcome of a race. Five-time winner Bernard Hinault (far right) was leading the 1985 Tour when this shot was taken, and eventually won.

stop Henri Anglade from winning. The next year Anglade was off to a good start when Rivière joined a break that wrecked the field and won the race— for Gastone Nencini. Rivière claimed to have joined the break to slow it down, but this was not supported by photos of him at the front, riding as if possessed.

Vietto never won the Tour. He was second in 1939 and returned when the event resumed in 1947, 13 years after his sacrifice. He took the lead in the Alps, defended it in the Pyrenees, but lost it to Pierre Brambilla during an 87-mile time trial. Brambilla held it until the final stage, which included a hill called Bonsecours—good help—but it's doubtful that he would agree with the name. Jean Robic attacked on that hill, chasing the prize to be won at the top and unaware that Lucien Teisseire was already ahead with a small break. When Robic looked around Brambilla was nowhere to be seen. Robic later stated that he intended only to get to the top first, but upon seeing Teisseire decided to carry on to the break. In Paris, Robic had gained 13 minutes over Brambilla and won the race without having worn the yellow jersey.

Foreigners won the Tour for the next five years—Fausto Coppi twice, Gino Bartali, and the two Swiss, Ferdi Kubler and Hugo Koblet. In 1949

Coppi demolished the field on the Izoard then waited to give Bartali the stage as a birthday present. Hugo Koblet dominated the Tour in 1951. At the end of the stage that won him the race, he carefully freewheeled a mile from the line in order to comb his hair and straighten his jersey.

Abdel Kader Zaaf also made his mark on the Tour in 1951. Refused permission by his captain to break away and win a stage, Zaaf swore to wreck the race. He attacked savagely, dropping an unwell Coppi and the entire field. It's claimed that once his lead was safe, he dismounted and went for a drink or two of wine. Imagine the surprise felt by all when Zaaf emerged from the hostelry where he had slaked his thirst and raced the wrong way into the peloton.

Then came Louison Bobet. Not an outstanding climber, he was only an average sprinter and initially poor at time trials, yet he won every type of stage. If ever there was a self-made rider it was Bobet. Thijs won the Tour three times but Bobet was the first to do so in consecutive years.

Bobet took his first Tour in 1953 over the Izoard Pass, coming from behind to drop the field for a lead he kept until the end. The second win was quite easy but the third was a desperate affair. A member of Bobet's team had taken a 12-minute lead and didn't intend to relinquish it. Charly Gaul, the new climbing sensation, was fourth overall with the Mont Ventoux to come. On its pitiless slopes Kubler attacked with Gaul on his wheel. Bobet had no choice but to chase and Gaul, the Angel of the Mountain, was dropped on the hardest climb of the race. Bobet won the stage and took the overall lead a few days later, but had to work to keep it all the way to Paris.

Anquetil seemed the complete antithesis of Bobet. Anquetil was cool and calculating, with a magnificent physique, almost unbelievable strength and determination, and a degree of class that few have ever matched. Anquetil's usual method was to establish his position then defend it, but his 1963 victory included a stage victory over Federico Bahamontes on the vital day in the Alps.

Raymond Poulidor first rode the Tour in 1962 and his last entry was in 1976. In those years his finishing positions were 3rd, 8th, 2nd, 2nd, 3rd, 9th, dnf, 3rd, 7th, dns, 3rd, dnf, 2nd, 19th, and 3rd. Poulidor should have won in 1964 and a mixture of selfish riding by a colleague and sheer misfortune cost him the race in 1968. In 1964 Anquetil emerged from the Alps in second, 31 seconds ahead of Poulidor. After a rest day in Andorra it became obvious that Anquetil was far from himself. Up the long Envalira climb out of Andorra he lost four minutes to a lead group that included Poulidor and Bahamontes. In between were the race leader and the leader of the points competition. Flanked by two of his lieutenants, Anquetil struggled to the top, forced himself to attack down the other side and caught the intermediate riders. Then the chase was on. Had Poulidor known Anquetil's condition he might have doubled the gap but it was too late. Ten miles from the finish Poulidor had a dreadful wheel change and lost 30 seconds on a stage that he could have won by minutes. But he was to have a second chance.

A week later little had changed except that the former race leader had vanished and Anquetil was in yellow. The stage finish was at the top of the Puy-de-Dome, one of the most savage climbs in France. The leaders were together at the foot. Julio Jimenez and Bahamontes were fighting for King of the Mountains and were first to jump. Poulidor failed to respond. Not until half a mile from the top did he tear himself away from Anquetil. While Jimenez gained 1:39 on Anquetil, Poulidor managed only half a minute. Anquetil won the Tour by 55 seconds over the man who was afraid to attack him.

Similar indecision appeared to cost Poulidor the race in 1965, but the truth was that Félice Gimondi was untouchable. It was not until 1968 that Poulidor again looked a likely winner. In 1967 Roger Pingeon had won due to a long solo break in the North and the subsequent unselfish help from his team, Poulidor included. In 1968 when the race left the Pyrenees Poulidor was fourth overall, 4:13 from the leader, while Pingeon was more than seven minutes down. Pingeon embarked upon another marathon break that earned him three minutes and an eventual fifth place in Paris. Meanwhile Poulidor was left in the bunch until, in the usual panic near the end of a stage when the pace increases and the lead diminishes, he was knocked off his bike by a member of the motorcycle convoy and his race was over. Perhaps Poulidor should have imitated Bobet who retired forever from the Tour some years earlier at the top of the Iseran Pass, then the highest in Europe at 9,088 feet. (The 9,193-foot Col de la Bonnette has subseqeuntly been opened.) It was typical of Bobet that he should quit at the summit. It was typical of Poulidor that he kept riding the Tour and six years later was Eddy Merckx's closest challenger.

Jan Janssen ultimately won the 1968 race, overhauling Herman van Springel in the final time trial. But it was really the death of Tom Simpson on the Mont Ventoux in the year before that gave Janssen his victory. Reacting almost hysterically against accusations that the 1967 Tour had been murderously hard—which it hadn't—the organizers designed a 1968 race in which the top four finishers—Janssen, van Springel, Ferdinand Bracke, and Gregorio San Miguel—were riders who ordinarily would have little chance of such high positions.

But all was put right in 1969. Janssen and van Springel finished 53 and 70 minutes down on Merckx, the first Belgian winner since 1939. Merckx had won the 1968 Giro, taking the points and climbing titles for good measure. He came to the Tour for the first time in 1969 and attacked for

Eddy Merckx is one of only three riders to win the Tour five times. Perhaps the greatest cyclist ever, Merckx had a reputation for making things tough on his competitors. He's shown here leading Felice Gimondi (left) in the 1969 Tour, which Merckx won by more than 16 minutes.

three weeks. Here's an illustration of Merckx's dominance. In a previous year Bahamontes led over the Aubisque Pass by seven minutes and arrived at Pau with a two-minute lead. In 1969 Merckx led over the Aubisque by eight minutes and, following a similar route, doubled it to 16 between the summit and the finish.

For two years Merckx was unchallenged, winning whatever classification he chose, but 1971 was different. An almost unknown Alpine village called Orcieres-Merlette had put in a successful bid to host a stage finish, gambling on the chance for publicity. There have been few more successful gambles in pro cycling. The story began on the Puy-de-Dome where Luis Ocana dared to attack Merckx, who was forced to let him go and trailed in fourth for the stage behind Joop Zoetemelk and Joaquim Agostinho. Two days later Merckx, in a lead group of six, punctured in the Chartreuse hills. It was unusual that he never got back to the front, but the Belgian fans were confident that he would be back to form the next day on the long climb to Orcieres.

On the very first climb of the day José-Manuel Fuente attacked and was quickly joined by Agostinho. Ocana, Zoetemelk and Lucien van Impe got up to the pair and dropped them on the twisting descent. For many miles the three stayed together until, 40 miles from the finish, Ocana attacked on the Col de Noyer and dropped his companions. Merckx eventually caught Zoetemelk, but Ocana continued relentlessly. At Ocieres he had taken an amazing six minutes from van Impe and almost nine from Merckx. Was the Tour ready to crown a new champion? Sadly, we were destined never to find out.

Merckx recovered a little of the lost time the next day, then awaited the Pyrenees, where Ocana took a heavy fall and was forced to quit. The next year Merckx won again and Ocana had to wait for victory until 1973 when Merckx didn't ride. Merckx won again in 1974 but, in my opinion, his greatest-ever ride was in 1975.

Merckx had been winning big races for almost 10 seasons, never sparing himself. By 1975, although still capable of winning classics, the punch had gone. Nevertheless, he wanted a record sixth Tour victory and was prepared to fight for it. Merckx was in his usual yellow and all was going well with him until the Puy-de-Dome. Near the summit, a spectator punched him viciously in the kidneys. Van Impe and Bernard Thévenet were able to ride away, but Merckx still held the overall lead. After a rest day the field faced five climbs on the way from Nice to Pra-Loup. Merckx countered every hostile move, led the way over the third pass, and attacked on the fourth to

Thanks in part to 7–Eleven—the first U.S. pro road team to compete on the Continent—more Americans are riding professionally in Europe than ever. Shown here in the team time trial of the 1987 Tour are (from left) Davis Phinney, Dag-Otto Lauritzen (a Norwegian), Bob Roll, Jonathan Boyer (obscured), Jeff Bradley, Ron Kiefel (obscured), Andy Hampsten, Jeff Pierce, and, at the right, Raul Alcala (a Mexican).

go clear by a few seconds. On the descent he added slightly to his lead. But he faced a four-mile climb to Pra-Loup. First Gimondi caught him, then Thévenet went past everyone to win the stage.

The next day had three more steep climbs and Merckx wasn't finished. Attacking on the descent from the first pass, he approached the Izoard clear, but the effort was too much—particularly for a man having difficulty breathing because of his injury. Thévenet again caught and dropped him, crossing the Izoard first as tradition demands of a winner. Two days later, Merckx crashed and fractured a cheek bone, but still he did not give up. At the finish in Paris, Thévenet's overall margin of victory was a little under three minutes and he praised second-place Merckx for his courage. Merckx, statesmanlike in defeat, said that he owed it to Thévenet that he had reached the finish.

After Merckx it was Hinault's turn to win five times. King of the time trial, often alone in the mountains, Hinault was as unbeatable as Merckx had been at his best, and most dangerous when his pride was wounded. In 1979 Hinault won the last two stages, including a marvelous Champs Élysées finish in which he and Zoetemelk, GC leaders, dropped the field to arrive together. In 1981 Hinault was being written off as not being a climber—with one mountain stage left a foolish thing for any critic to write. Allowing an early break to form, Hinault bided his time, launching the counterattack with two climbs to go. On the first he caught all but two members of the break. On the last he dropped the two to finish more than two minutes clear. Despite dreadful knee injuries and a miserable time for two years Hinault came back to win again in 1985. It was his fifth victory, and a narrow one that might have been more difficult but for the misfortunes which befell teammate Greg LeMond.

Hinault's final Tour came in 1986. Having said that he would help LeMond win, he seemed to have a strange way of giving help. Hinault attacked repeatedly and subsequently claimed that this was necessary in order for LeMond to prove himself worthy of victory, which the American surely did. LeMond was the first from outside of Europe to win the Tour.

A gunshot wound sustained while hunting kept LeMond from entering the Tour in 1987, throwing the race wide open and giving Stephen Roche the chance to complete a remarkable double of the Giro and the Tour. The Tour was dominated by the struggle between Roche and Pedro Delgado, a struggle in which both riders acquitted themselves with honor and distinction. But a word must be said about using team time trials as part of individual GC. Roche finally beat Delgado by 40 seconds in 115 hours of racing. In the TTT Roche's Carrera team beat Delgado's P.D.M. team by 1:01 or, to put it another way, Roche took 1:01 from Delgado through a

In 1986, Greg LeMond became the first U.S. rider to win the Tour. This hilly 13th stage in the Pyrenees was the first LeMond won that year, but he was still 40 seconds short of wresting the leader's yellow jersey from Bernard Hinault. From left: Claude Criquielion, LeMond, Andy Hampsten (another U.S. rider, who placed fourth overall), Hinault, and Luis Herrera.

team exercise. Who is to say how much each rider contributed to his team's time? All one can say is that Delgado should have lost to Roche on individual times alone.

Delgado got revenge in 1988, winning the Tour and adding almost 1 kph to the speed record set by Hinault in 1981. But his win was marred by the revelation that he had used artificial stimulants. There is no defense for doping, but Delgado's victory might not have been questioned if the Tour organization and the lab hadn't leaked the fact that he had tested positive for a substance which was not banned by the Union Cycliste Internationale.

Delgado was easily the best rider in the Tour. His training program was perfectly calculated to bring him to peak at the right time, and he dominated the race despite good efforts by Steven Rooks and others. Delgado took the lead as, and when, he was expected, adding to it almost at will until the mountain stages were over.

It was the fastest Tour ever, largely because it was one of the easiest for years, probably since 1968, when the route was made ridiculously easy in reaction to Simpson's death the year before. What made the 1988 race so fast was the very low average stage mileage, a factor which is far more important to most riders than the number of mountain passes.

KING OF THE MOUNTAINS

1933	Trueba (Sp)	**1957**	Nencini (I)	**1974**	Perurena (Sp)
1934	Vietto (F)	**1958**	Bahamontes (Sp)	**1975**	van Impe (B)
1935	Vervaecke (B)	**1959**	Bahamontes (Sp)	**1976**	Bellini (I)
1936	Berrendero (Sp)	**1960**	Massignan (I)	**1977**	van Impe (B)
1937	Vervaecke (B)	**1961**	Massignan (I)	**1978**	Martinez (F)
1938	Bartali (I)	**1962**	Bahamontes (Sp)	**1979**	Battaglin (I)
1939	Maes, S. (B)	**1963**	Bahamontes (Sp)	**1980**	Martin (F)
1947	Brambilla (F)	**1964**	Bahamontes (Sp)	**1981**	van Impe (B)
1948	Bartali (I)	**1965**	Jimenez (Sp)	**1982**	Vallet (F)
1949	Coppi (I)	**1966**	Jimenez (Sp)	**1983**	van Impe (B)
1950	Bobet (F)	**1967**	Jimenez (Sp)	**1984**	Millar (GB)
1951	Géminiani (F)	**1968**	Gonzalez (Sp)	**1985**	Herrera (Co)
1952	Coppi (I)	**1969**	Merckx (B)	**1986**	Hinault (F)
1953	Lorono (Sp)	**1970**	Merckx (B)	**1987**	Herrera (Co)
1954	Bahamontes (Sp)	**1971**	van Impe (B)	**1988**	Rooks (Nl)
1955	Gaul (L)	**1972**	van Impe (B)		
1956	Gaul (L)	**1973**	Torres (Sp)		

POINTS WINNER

1953	Schaer (Sw)	**1965**	Janssen (Nl)	**1977**	Esclassan (F)
1954	Kubler (Sw)	**1966**	Planckaert, W. (B)	**1978**	Maertens (B)
1955	Ockers (B)	**1967**	Janssen (Nl)	**1979**	Hinault (F)
1956	Ockers (B)	**1968**	Bitossi (I)	**1980**	Pévenage (B)
1957	Forestier (F)	**1969**	Merckx (B)	**1981**	Maertens (B)
1958	Graczyk (F)	**1970**	Godefroot (B)	**1982**	Kelly (Ir)
1959	Darrigade (F)	**1971**	Merckx (B)	**1983**	Kelly (Ir)
1960	Graczyk (F)	**1972**	Merckx (B)	**1984**	Hoste (B)
1961	Darrigade (F)	**1973**	van Springel (B)	**1985**	Kelly (Ir)
1962	Altig (WG)	**1974**	Sercu (B)	**1986**	Vanderaerden (B)
1963	van Looy (B)	**1975**	van Linden (B)	**1987**	van Poppel (Nl)
1964	Janssen (Nl)	**1976**	Maertens (B)	**1988**	van Poppel (Nl)

1914	Rheinwald (Sw)
1915–16	not held
1917	Martinet (F)
1918	Sieger (Sw)
1919	Suter (Sw)
1920	Suter (Sw)
1921	Maffeo (I)
1922	Suter (Sw)
1923	Muschke (G)
1924	Suter (Sw)
1925	Kaspar (Sw)
1926	Blattmann (Sw)
1927	Notter (Sw)
1928	Suter (Sw)
1929	Suter (Sw)
1930	Taverne (B)
1931	Bulla (Au)
1932	Erne (Sw)
1933	Blattmann (Sw)
1934	Egli (Sw)
1935	Egli (Sw)
1936	Buchwalder (Sw)
1937	Amberg (Sw)
1938	Martin (Sw)
1939	Litschi (Sw)
1940	Zimmermann (Sw)
1941	Diggelmann (Sw)

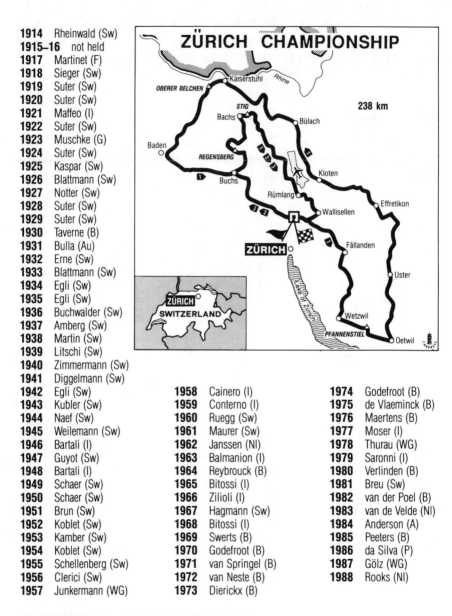

ZÜRICH CHAMPIONSHIP

238 km

1942	Egli (Sw)	1958	Cainero (I)	1974	Godefroot (B)
1943	Kubler (Sw)	1959	Conterno (I)	1975	de Vlaeminck (B)
1944	Naef (Sw)	1960	Ruegg (Sw)	1976	Maertens (B)
1945	Weilemann (Sw)	1961	Maurer (Sw)	1977	Moser (I)
1946	Bartali (I)	1962	Janssen (NI)	1978	Thurau (WG)
1947	Guyot (Sw)	1963	Balmanion (I)	1979	Saronni (I)
1948	Bartali (I)	1964	Reybrouck (B)	1980	Verlinden (B)
1949	Schaer (Sw)	1965	Bitossi (I)	1981	Breu (Sw)
1950	Schaer (Sw)	1966	Zilioli (I)	1982	van der Poel (B)
1951	Brun (Sw)	1967	Hagmann (Sw)	1983	van de Velde (NI)
1952	Koblet (Sw)	1968	Bitossi (I)	1984	Anderson (A)
1953	Kamber (Sw)	1969	Swerts (B)	1985	Peeters (B)
1954	Koblet (Sw)	1970	Godefroot (B)	1986	da Silva (P)
1955	Schellenberg (Sw)	1971	van Springel (B)	1987	Gölz (WG)
1956	Clerici (Sw)	1972	van Neste (B)	1988	Rooks (NI)
1957	Junkermann (WG)	1973	Dierickx (B)		

SPEED RECORD: Gino Bartali, 42.228 kph in 1946
MOST VICTORIES: Henri Suter, 6

Zürich Championship

The name Zürich Championship is slightly misleading because there are actually several races on the same day—schoolboys, juniors, amateurs, and professionals—with a grand total of more than 1,000 entries in most years. The pro race is held in Zürich and Aargau Provinces, with the start and finish often outside the Zürich velodrome, and a final finish circuit of around 25 miles. In 1988 the race moved from early May to mid August to accommodate other changes in the calendar, and both it and the finish circuit were shortened.

A glance at the list of Zürich Championship winners shows the typical pattern of domination by home riders followed by internationalization of the race in the last 20 years or so. It also shows a lot of unfamiliar names, for many of the Swiss winners have never won another major race except possibly the Tour of Switzerland. This is largely because the Swiss, in keeping with that peculiar independence that has characterized them for so long, preferred to ride every type of race within their own frontiers rather than specialize and travel widely in one discipline.

One such all-rounder was Oscar Egg. While an apprentice draftsman in Paris, Egg read of the great riders of the day and was prompted to buy his first bicycle. Five years later, in 1912, he broke the world hour record. He broke it twice more before the start of World War I, whereupon he returned to Switzerland and won the national road and sprint championships. Subsequent victories included Paris-Tours and stage wins in the Tour de France and Tour of Italy (Giro). But he remained greatest on the track, winning the Swiss sprint championship regularly for 12 years. He set the world record for distance in a six-day, was a brilliant tandem rider, and at one time or another beat most of the specialists in motorpaced racing.

Egg's eclectic approach was widely copied, but his willingness to travel outside Switzerland to race was not. Until the arrival of Ferdi Kubler and Hugo Koblet relatively few Swiss riders traveled regularly to France or

Gino Bartali's 25–year cycling career was one of the longest. He was a preeminent climber, taking seven King of the Mountains titles in the Giro, which he won three times, and two Mountains titles and two overall wins in the Tour. His 1946 speed record in the Zürich Championship— 42.228 kph—still stands.

Italy, though Henri Suter, Zürich record holder with six victories, won classics in France and Belgium.

There is little to write about the early years of the race. It is worth noting that the record speed has stood for more than 40 years. Gino Bartali rode frequently in Switzerland, partly because it was not too far from his home, partly because it allowed good acclimatization before the Giro and partly because he was always made very welcome. When he beat Fausto Coppi in Zürich in 1946, he could hardly have dreamed that his record speed of 26.24 mph would stand so long. Despite considerable improvements in equipment and roads over the past four decades there are many events, among them the world championship, with lower record speeds. Phil Anderson has come closest—within 1 mph—to breaking Bartali's Zürich record.

Not even the might of the great Belgian road sprinters could reach Bartali's speed. But their presence in 1975 brought tremendous interest,

particularly during the final sprint of a dozen riders that almost brought Eddy Merckx and Francesco Moser to blows. Zürich is one of the few races that Merckx never won, but he certainly tried that year, indulging in a bit of elbow work with Moser and ignoring Roger de Vlaeminck's sprint to victory down the other side of the road. The top riders were all back the following year for another tumultuous sprint finish that Freddy Maertens won from de Vlaeminck.

One of the great upsets occurred in 1981 and brought two relative unknowns into prominence. Neither has since achieved much of note, but that day they looked like future world champions. Henri Rinklin made a suicidal attack on the first hill in the Henniger Tower Grand Prix a day or two earlier, and stayed away for 50 miles. He did it again in Zürich, attacking after only 20 miles, and was joined shortly by Béat Breu. Their lead reached 18 minutes before the bunch reacted, but by then it was too late—barely. Five miles from the line the gap was down to just under a minute and Rinklin was almost on his knees. To his credit Breu waited for his fellow fugitive, nursed him to within sight of the line, then took off to win by two seconds. The bunch came in half a minute later.

Later that year Breu won the Tour of Switzerland in impressive style and was in a position to threaten Giovanni Battaglin in the Giro, but eventually finished 10th.

The 1982 race might have introduced a new nationality to the list of winners, but Eric MacKenzie of New Zealand failed the dope test and was disqualified. MacKenzie can turn his track speed, acquired in Belgium, to good use on the road. Although many see him as a future star, he still has to confirm his early promise. Another of whom this is true is Acacio da Silva of Portugal, the second rider of quality from that country. Da Silva won Zürich in 1986, breaking away from a small group in the closing miles. Canadian Steve Bauer took second, as he had done a few days earlier in Frankfurt. With Michael Wilson, an Australian, third in Frankfurt and American Greg LeMond fifth in Zürich, it is clear that riders from English-speaking nations are serious contenders on the European circuit.

1927	Binda (I)	**1952**	Müller (WG)	**1971**	Merckx (B)
1928	Ronsse (B)	**1953**	Coppi (I)	**1972**	Basso (I)
1929	Ronsse (B)	**1954**	Bobet (F)	**1973**	Gimondi (I)
1930	Binda (I)	**1955**	Ockers (B)	**1974**	Merckx (B)
1931	Guerra (I)	**1956**	van Steenbergen (B)	**1975**	Kuiper (NI)
1932	Binda (I)	**1957**	van Steenbergen (B)	**1976**	Maertens (B)
1933	Speicher (F)	**1958**	Baldini (I)	**1977**	Moser (I)
1934	Kaers (B)	**1959**	Darrigade (F)	**1978**	Knetemann (NI)
1935	Aerts (B)	**1960**	van Looy (B)	**1979**	Raas (NI)
1936	Magne (F)	**1961**	van Looy (B)	**1980**	Hinault (F)
1937	Meulenberg (B)	**1962**	Stablinski (F)	**1981**	Maertens (B)
1938	Kint (B)	**1963**	Beheyt (B)	**1982**	Saronni (I)
1939–45	not held	**1964**	Janssen (NI)	**1983**	LeMond (US)
1946	Knecht (Sw)	**1965**	Simpson (GB)	**1984**	Criquielion (B)
1947	Middelkamp (NI)	**1966**	Altig (WG)	**1985**	Zoetemelk (NI)
1948	Schotte (B)	**1967**	Merckx (B)	**1986**	Argentin (I)
1949	van Steenbergen (B)	**1968**	Adorni (I)	**1987**	Roche (Ir)
1950	Schotte (B)	**1969**	Ottenbros (NI)	**1988**	Fondriest (I)
1951	Kubler (Sw)	**1970**	Monsere (B)		

SPEED RECORD: Joop Zoetemelk, 41.501 kph in 1985
MOST VICTORIES: Alfredo Binda, Rik van Steenbergen, and Eddy Merckx, 3 each

World Professional Road Championship

After the Tour de France, European cycling enters a phase of criterium racing. Though the criteriums are rich pickings for the most successful Tour riders, who can have a contract for every racing day, they also present problems. Because they are often far apart, many hours are spent traveling by car. Appearance money is willingly paid to stars, who are expected to justify it, not necessarily by winning everywhere but at least by turning up and racing.

The world championship offers another change, being the only race of the season contested by national teams in national jerseys. Professional team sponsors dislike this, since they pay the riders' wages, and they are ready with their commercial stickers to go on the rainbow jersey the moment the identity of the new champion is known. Although the traditional cycling nations have dominated the worlds, Great Britain, the United States, and Ireland have all had riders win the coveted title. In my experience the Dutch and Italians are the best organized. The ongoing feuds in Italy and the dearth of outstanding Dutch riders rarely prevent a fine team performance. Belgium occasionally rides as a team, but more often as a collection of individuals, and France never seems to present a homogeneous outfit.

The sponsors are not the only detractors of the championships. A frequent argument is that to determine a world champion on the basis of one race is unjust. Such critics point to the likes of 1969 world champion Armin Ottenbros and ask how such a mediocre rider could be called champion of the world. The simple answer is that he won the title by beating everyone in the race. Some feel that, as in some other sports, a season-long competition (like the Pernod Trophy in cycling) should be used to determine the champion. But while consistent performances are meritorious, the Pernod could have been won by a large collection of *places d'honneur*. The world title should go to the rider who can lift himself above the others on a single day and in a race format that remains distinctive. The world championship, usually held on the last Sunday in August or the first Sunday in September and comprising 17 or 18 laps of a 10-mile circuit, meets those requirements.

The idea of a world road championship was first advanced in 1898. Although world track championships had been held since 1893, it wasn't until 1921 that the amateur road championship was introduced. It was a time trial, but was replaced by a conventional road race in 1923.

Finally, in 1927, Italian pressure was rewarded with the creation of the championship as we know it. When the first world professional road

Unlike most famous events, the world championship is held in a different location each year. It's also the only race of the European season in which professional riders doff their sponsors' logos in favor of national team jerseys. Here, riders pass through a feed zone during the 1987 championships at Villach, Austria.

championship took place in Germany on the Nurburgring, the winner was, appropriately, an Italian.

The amateurs and pros raced together that year, but with separate classifications. While France selected four amateurs and one professional, Italy had the all-professional lineup of Alfredo Binda, Costante Girardengo, Gaetano Belloni, and Domenico Piemontese. Halfway through the race it was raining heavily. The combination of hills and rain repeatedly cut the field to shreds, but the top riders managed to claw their way back to the front on each occasion. With six laps to go Belloni launched the Italian offensive, followed by Piemontese and then Girardengo. Binda got up to them both, with three amateurs. The Italians worked perfectly as a team, picking off the amateurs one by one. Binda jumped 20 miles from the finish and the real race was over. Girardengo finished second, 7:15 behind, and Piemontese third, with Belloni emerging from the rags and tatters of the bunch to take fourth.

The following year at Budapest, Hungary, riders of other nations were determined to stop Binda. Three broke away from the start of the now all-pro event. Ferdinand le Drogo punctured and lost the lead for good, but Jules van Hevel and Georges Ronsse worked perfectly together, until van Hevel ran into a cow and was unable to continue. The Italian team quit the race and Ronsse won by almost 20 minutes.

The rivalry between Italians and Belgians overshadowed the championship for the next four years. In 1929 Ronsse outsprinted Nicolas Frantz and Binda. The following year on a hilly loop in the Ardennes, Binda recruited Learco Guerra, the so-called human locomotive. Binda and Ronsse dominated the race, despite a nasty moment when Binda hit a dog and fell off his bike. On the last two hills Binda dropped Ronsse but the Belgian came back each time. On the final lap they finessed like track sprinters, watching one another so closely that Guerra caught up and passed both of them. Only 10 yards from the line Binda forced his bike to the front and won. The next year saw a time trial championship which Guerra dominated, but Binda was back for his third win in 1932—this time in Italy. Binda probably remains the only champion not to have crossed the finish line. Having disposed of Remo Bertoni and Romain Gijssels, his last two challengers, Binda was mobbed yards short of the line by his fans on the Frascati circuit.

The 1933 championship took place in France and the team selectors horrified the French public by omitting Georges Speicher, who had won the Tour a few weeks earlier. Roger Lapébie, Antonin Magne, and Paul Chocque were chosen. On the eve of the race Chocque took ill, but where was Speicher? He had not been seen for days. Eventually he was found at the movies and told he was on the team. Less than 24 hours later he was the first to win the Tour and the worlds in the same season, after dominating from beginning to end and winning by more than five minutes.

The next world champion was a track specialist specially chosen to suit the course. Karel Kaers was selected when the Belgians realized that the 1934 Leipzig circuit was completely flat and offered no opportunity for the strong riders to escape. They were right. They were right again the next year in picking Jean Aerts, amateur champion eight years earlier, who rode away to finish three minutes clear. Australian Hubert Oppermann, probably the first native speaker of English to enjoy a successful career as a European pro, finished seventh.

In 1936 Magne restored French pride. On a 4.5-mile circuit near Berne, Switzerland, he split the field with an attack after 20 miles, and dropped all but two others with another attack at the feed, 40 miles from the finish.

Fausto Coppi was one of the all-time greats. He is tied with Alfredo Binda and Eddy Merckx for the most wins in the Giro d'Italia, at five, and is the only rider with that many wins in the Tour of Lombardy. A successful all-rounder, Coppi won Milan–San Remo three times and the Tour de France twice, and was world champion.

Attacking again with 10 miles to go, he won by 9:27—gaining almost a minute per mile after that final attack. An unknown Dutchman, Theo Middelkamp, was third.

The Belgians replied in the next two years with Eloi Meulenberg and Marcel Kint, who took sprint victories. Swiss Hans Knecht, who had won the amateur championship in 1938, the last worlds held before the war, returned in 1946 to add the pro title on his home roads near Zürich. He escaped at the foot of the last hill to win by 10 seconds from Kint and Rik van Steenbergen, who were preoccupied with the forthcoming sprint. The inquests were numerous. It was alleged that an unknown hand had seized Kint's saddle as he began to chase Knecht. It was alleged that Kint and van Steenbergen had come to a financial agreement, but nothing could be proved. The following year was no more satisfactory. Van Steenbergen, Fausto Coppi, and Ferdi Kubler retired half way and the crown went to that unknown from 1936, Middelkamp.

Belgians dominated for the next three years, Briek Schotte taking two around van Steenbergen's 1949 win. Controversy returned in 1952, when the Luxembourg location implied a race with climbs. The opposite was true, with the only hill a slight rise on the finish circuit. Adolphe Deledda and Willy Kemp were clear of the field with a mile to go when Deledda refused to do any more work, afraid of being outsprinted by the local hero. Van Steenbergen, Louison Bobet and the bunch swallowed them up and it seemed likely that the greats would fight for the title. But that sole hill proved their undoing. Sprinting in top gear and with a slight headwind, they found their strength insufficient and they were overhauled by a group of unknowns in a lower gear. Heinz Müller became champion and, after a brief contract with a French team that brought him little satisfaction, returned to the Black Forest and opened a bicycle shop.

The next three years restored the reputation of the race. 1953 had been a difficult year for Coppi. Thirty-four years old and never world champion, he had been attacked in the Catholic press for his adulterous relationship with a woman always known as the White Lady. In the Giro there had been a misunderstanding with Hugo Koblet, one of Coppi's closest friends. After Koblet caught Coppi during a descent in the Dolomites, Coppi congratulated him on winning the race. Koblet took this as a nonaggression pact, but Coppi's manager insisted that Coppi do something to counter the hostile press. Over the Stelvio Pass, Coppi attacked against his own wishes, dropping Koblet and winning the race. That evening when Coppi tried to explain, Koblet slammed the door in his face.

Coppi refused to ride the Tour de France that year, but instead planned a desperate bid for the worlds. He went to Lugano, the site of the race, and trained seven hours a day. It was to be Charly Gaul's first great performance. Attacking again and again on the hilly circuit Gaul split the field repeatedly. Only a dozen riders remained with him 50 miles from the finish, but Gaul had dipped too deeply into his reserves. Now it was Coppi's turn and he attacked, riding away to win by six minutes.

The next year belonged to Bobet, although he was convinced that he could not beat Coppi. Robert Varnajo and Michele Gismondi made a long and suicidal break. When Bobet attacked he took Jacques Anquetil, Gaul, Fritz Schär, and, inevitably, Coppi. Varnajo and Gismondi quickly disappeared, then Anquetil found the pace too much, but Gaul and Coppi hung on. Schär didn't count. The next attack, on the steepest part of the circuit in Solingen, Germany, saw Coppi in trouble, spinning his back wheel and almost falling, with Gaul trapped behind him. Coppi did not attempt to catch Bobet and Gaul couldn't, but Schär was still there.

Clear of opposition, Bobet and Schär approached the grandstand and the pits to start the last lap. Eighty yards past the pits, where the mechanics were putting away their tools and spares, Bobet punctured. Fortunately one mechanic had seen the mishap. He grabbed a bike, sprinted up to Bobet with a front wheel, and Bobet was away again. But Schär was out of sight. Bobet caught the courageous Swiss on the last hill with just over a mile to go, attacked immediately, and came home in triumph. Schär, who had outridden Anquetil, Coppi, Gaul, and the rest, followed at 12 seconds.

Rik van Steenbergen (right) took his third and final world championship in 1957 in Waregem, Belgium, with a sprint victory over Louison Bobet. Van Steenbergen was a great all-rounder, and one of only three riders to win the world professional road championship three times.

1955 was Stan Ockers' year. Eight minutes behind at the halfway point, he recovered to win alone by a minute. Van Steenbergen made his hat trick with sprint victories in 1956 and 1957.

Bobet was back for another try in 1958, but it was probably Coppi who cost him a second title at Rheims, France, that year. Bobet attacked after only 20 miles and was joined by Gastone Nencini and Gerrit Voorting. Such early breaks rarely succeed, but Coppi obviously believed that this one would. Unable to bridge the gap himself, he sent up Ercole Baldini, who caught the three. After Bobet had shaken off Nencini and Voorting, Baldini in turn got rid of Bobet with 20 miles to go. Instead of quitting Bobet characteristically rode on to finish second.

Sprints decided the next three championships, with André Darrigade winning once and Rik van Looy twice. It should have been Seamus Elliott at Salo, Italy, in 1962. Instigator of the vital attack, Elliott was a close friend of teammate Jean Stablinski. They had promised not to attack each other in the title race and when Elliott broke away Stablinski kept his word—for the moment. Jos Hoevenaars set off after Elliott and Stablinski, deciding that the title was no longer safe, sat on Hoevenaars' wheel until Elliott was caught. Two laps from the end Stablinski went away alone and looked a certain champion until he punctured out of reach of the pits. But the judges allowed Stablinski to borrow a spectator's bike—several sizes too large—and he stayed away for the win.

More has been written about the 1963 championship, held in Ronse, Flanders, than any other. Van Looy wanted his third title and the Belgian team—allegedly all in his pay for the day—had been picked to help him win. As the race neared the finish his success seemed assured, with Belgians controlling everything and everybody. Van Looy asked Benoni Beheyt to lead out the sprint, but Beheyt claimed to have cramp in his calf. Raymond Poulidor attacked on the last lap and was brought back. On the last hill Tom Simpson had a go and van Looy chased. He caught Simpson 500 yards from the line with the pack breathing down his neck. Should he ease or not, with the line so near and yet to far?

Van Looy carried on, Beheyt on one side and Armand Desmet on the other. Suddenly van Looy lost his line, moved across the track, and pushed Beheyt towards the rail. Beheyt put out a hand, to hold van Looy back according to some, to stop himself from falling according to others. Beheyt stopped pedaling, but at the line his front wheel was marginally in front of van Looy's. It is said that van Looy never spoke to him again and it is certain that Beheyt never won another major race, but the chief commissaire insisted that van Looy would have been disqualified had he crossed the line first. Van Looy never did manage a third title.

The worlds finally made the British headlines in 1965. An early attack took several dangerous riders away. Barry Hoban joined the break as watchdog, while Alan Ramsbottom and Vin Denson paced Simpson up to the lead. For several laps the break was consolidated, then the weaker members began to drop. Hoban was still doing a marvelous job of protecting Simpson, who was getting sick of the drafters in the group. Simpson attacked uphill with two laps to go and only Rudi Altig went with him. Old friends, they worked well together, though Altig asked Simpson not to push so hard up the hills. As they rode the last lap they reached an agreement that they would separate at the kilometer board, neither trying to shelter behind the other in a tactical sprint.

In *Cycling is my Life* (Stanley Paul, 1966), Simpson recounts the finish. "I started my sprint a few hundred yards out and kept going as hard as I could. I was looking down, looking for his shadow on the road as he came up on me. I kept thinking, 'He's coming! He's coming! He's coming!' And suddenly when I was ten yards from the line it dawned on me. 'He hasn't! He hasn't made it! It's mine!' and I was over the line, grinning like a maniac, heart pounding and tears welling in my eyes."

Altig won the following year in front of a home crowd in West Germany. He had missed the break and Anquetil, who earlier that summer had given the Tour to Lucien Aimar, looked every inch a world champion. Aimar made a late move to join the break, taking Altig, only to see Altig outsprint Anquetil for the title.

In 1967 Eddy Merckx won a five-man sprint for the first of his three world championship titles. In 1971 only Felice Gimondi could follow him to the line, and in 1974 Poulidor was the only one to stay with him to the end. Between times Merckx had mixed fortunes.

Whether he would have retained his title in 1968 will never be known. Despite the fact that competitors for the championship ride in national teams, Merckx, a Belgian, played the sponsors' game and allowed his trade teammate Vittorio Adorni to take an eight-minute victory in his native Italy. Again a domestique in 1969, Merckx sat back as Belgian Julien Stevens broke away with Dutchman Ottenbros on the Zolder, Belgium, course. The policy backfired when the Ottenbros became the most surprising, and no doubt surprised, world champion since Müller.

In 1970 Merckx came to Britain as road captain of the Belgian team. Scorning his own chances, he organized the race so well that every bunch arriving at the finish was led by a Belgian, with Jean-Pierre Monséré champion. Monséré died the following year when struck by a car during a criterium.

1972 was a year of serious miscalculation. Like Luxembourg, Gap, in the French Alps, should have provided a circuit that would favor the strong. Like Luxembourg, it did nothing of the sort. For most of the race Marino Basso rode on Merckx's wheel. Franco Bitossi jumped 400 yards from the line, but Merckx was ready. He led the counterattack, but realized that he was fractionally too late, for Bitossi was clear. Then Basso emerged, not from behind Merckx this time, but from behind an official car, and pipped Bitossi at the line. Merckx said later that he would have been happier to let Bitossi win the title.

Another Italian foiled Merckx at Barcelona in 1973, but what a different race. Merckx jumped hard from a group of seven or eight, dislodging several. Another Belgian, Freddy Maertens, brought up the rest, promising to lead out the sprint for Merckx but claiming to be incapable of taking second if Merckx broke away. Approaching the line on the last lap, Maertens waited for Merckx, who suddenly lost two lengths. Gimondi was on his pedals and clear in a flash, and outsprinted Merckx to win, with Maertens taking second. Merckx's 1974 title was his last.

In succeeding years Hennie Kuiper won a spectacular solo victory, Maertens outsprinted Francesco Moser, Moser in turn outsprinted Didi Thurau, and Gerrie Knetemann and Jan Raas gave the Netherlands two victories with Moser and Thurau second in respective years. The question that all France was asking was whether it would be Bernard Hinault's turn when the worlds returned to that country in 1980.

Hinault has always been able to respond to pressure. He was under enormous pressure in 1980, never having been world champion and knowing what was expected of him on home roads, albeit roads much closer to the homes of many Italian riders than to Hinault's native Brittany. Just as he was to justify French hopes in Paris-Roubaix, so he fulfilled expectations at the worlds, which were held on an excellent, hilly circuit at Sallanches in the Savoy Alps.

On the second lap Hinault was out in front with Johan de Muynck, but just to test the waters. As soon as they were back in the bunch, three others set off for 70 miles on their own. Hinault, Roger de Vlaeminck, and Joop Zoetemelk rode near the head of the main bunch throughout the race, content to control the gap and allow nobody else to escape. There had been brief showers and bright spells, but the rain intensified just after the three fugitives were caught. On the 12th and 13th laps Hinault attacked on the climb. Michel Pollentier and Gianbattista Baronchelli went with him, to be joined eventually by Robert Millar and Jörgen Marcussen. It was only a question of time, with Hinault attacking on the same hill every lap. One by one the riders with him were dropped—Pollentier on the 15th, Marcussen on the 17th, Millar on the 18th, and Baronchelli on the 20th, and final, lap.

There was neither pretense nor trickery, just a predictable attack on every lap until Hinault was left alone to ride to the finish. Baronchelli held his place to win the silver medal at 1:01 while the others fell back to the bunch from which Juan Fernandez won the sprint for third at 4:25, with Jonathan Boyer in fifth, then the best placing by an American.

Hinault was third the following year to Maertens whose first turn at the front began 200 yards from the line. In 1982 Hinault retired in mid race to the disgust of the British crowd and it was left to a brilliant Dutch team to try in vain to get Zoetemelk away. The finish was uphill and around a corner. Boyer broke just before the corner and looked a possible winner. But he went too soon. Greg LeMond misjudged the finish, chasing too soon and giving Saronni a flier. The uphill sprint was so fast that in the last 100 yards Saronni took five seconds from LeMond, who placed second.

The next year at Altenrhein, Switzerland, LeMond made amends, though not to Boyer. Annihilating Faustino Ruperez in the closing miles, LeMond finished alone, America's first professional road champion. After him came the unexpected win by Claude Criquielion in 1984 and then the unbelievable one in 1985 when Zoetemelk, attacking a mile from the line, held on to beat LeMond and a dozen others by three seconds. Moreno Argentin won a well-deserved victory in 1986 in the United States at Colorado Springs, attacking with 16 miles to go and shedding most of his companions, attacking again the following lap to dislodge all but Charly Mottet, and then comfortably winning the sprint.

1987 was Stephen Roche's year beyond question. Winner of the Giro after his attack on Roberto Visentini, winner of the Tour after his memorable battle with Pedro Delgado, Roche joined Coppi, Anquetil, Merckx, and Hinault—the five of them winners of both national tours in the same season. Merckx was the only rider to have won both stage races and the world title in the same year. The odds against Roche joining Merckx must have been hundreds to one. He was the marked man and in a very small team, one in which Sean Kelly was the only other rider of international class. With half a lap to go the odds had lengthened to thousands to one as Roche approached the finish in a bunch containing several of the best road sprinters in the world, Argentin and Kelly to name but two.

On the final lap a small group went clear, Roche covering the move for Kelly in the belief that Argentin would chase. When the gap was still about 200 yards entering the last mile and Kelly and Argentin were watching one another closely, Roche decided that the Irish hopes rested with him. Not usually a good sprinter, Roche surprised the others by sprinting past them with 500 yards to go. He held on to win by a single second, matching Merckx, with Argentin taking the sprint for second.

The favorites were nowhere to be seen in the 1988 world championship, held in Belgium. Mottet began the vital action, with Eddy Planckaert, surprisingly, an attacker. They were caught and passed by Criquielion and Maurizio Fondriest who, in turn, were caught by Canadian Steve Bauer with less than a mile to go. Des Fretwell, of *International Cycle Sport*, who was watching from the grandstand, judges that Criquielion tried to go through a gap that wasn't there. Bauer refused to let him through and the Belgian fell with the line in sight. Fondriest took advantage of Criquielion's fall and Bauer's lurch and got over the line first. Bauer was immediately disqualified—apparently with no official disciplinary hearing—and the other medals went to Martial Gayant, who was 27 seconds back, and Juan Fernandez, who had led in the chase group at 42 seconds.

1907 Garrigou (F)		
1908 Petit-Breton (F)		
1909 Faber (L)		
1910 Brocco (I)		
1911 Lapize (F)		
1912 Lapize (F)		
1913 Lapize (F)		
1914 Mottiat (B)		
1915–18 not held		
1919 Michiels (B)		
1920 Pélissier, H. (F)		
1921 Reboul (F)		
1922 Sellier (B)		
1923 Sellier (B)		
1924 Sellier (B)		
1925 Debaets (B)		
1926 Verschueren (B)		
1927 Frantz (L)		
1928 Ronsse (B)		
1929 Verhaegen (B)		
1930 Mottard (B)		
1931 Aerts (B)		
1932 Vervaecke (B)		
1933 Barthelemy (F)		
1934 Bonduel (B)		
1935 de Caluwe (B)		
1936 Meulenberg (B)	**1956** van Looy (B)	**1976** Gimondi (I)
1937 Beckaert (B)	**1957** van Daele (B)	**1977** Peeters, L. (B)
1938 Kint (B)	**1958** van Looy (B)	**1978** Raas (Nl)
1939 Bonduel (B)	**1959** Schoubben (B)	**1979** Peeters, L. (B)
1940–45 not held	**1960** Everaert (F)	**1980** Gavazzi (I)
1946 Schotte (B)	**1961** Cerami (B)	**1981** de Vlaeminck (I)
1947 Sterckx (B)	**1962** Wouters (B)	**1982** Hanegraaf (Nl)
1948 Poels (B)	**1963** Stablinski (F)	**1983** Prim (Sd)
1949 Diot (F)	**1964** van Coningsloo (B)	**1984** Vanderaerden (B)
1950 van Steenbergen (B)	**1965** Sels (B)	**1985** van der Poel (Nl)
1951 Gueguen (F)	**1966** Gimondi (B)	**1986** Bontempi (I)
1952 Schotte (B)	**1967–72** not held	**1987** Arras (B)
1953 Petrucci (I)	**1973** Merckx (B)	**1988** Gölz (WG)
1954 Hendrickx (B)	**1974** de Meyer (B)	
1955 Hendrickx (B)	**1975** Maertens (B)	

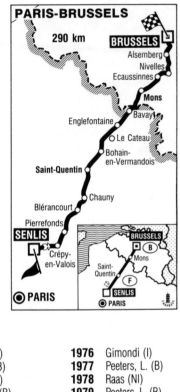

SPEED RECORD: Freddy Maertens, 46.11 kph in 1975
MOST VICTORIES: Octave Lapize and Félix Sellier, 3 each

Paris-Brussels

Few others than, perhaps, Octave Lapize, Felix Sellier, and Freddy Maertens would regard Paris-Brussels as their favorite race. It's the longest of the orthodox classics, often suffers from violent headwinds, and the route is grim for much of its length.

In a very short pro career Lapize won seven classics, the Tour de France, and was French road champion three times—as well as once at cyclocross. He actually took Paris-Brussels four times, being first over the line in 1910. But he and two others were disqualified for not observing a neutralized section midrace, and victory went to Maurice Brocco, who had been dropped by the break and dropped by the bunch, and had come back in the last two miles to take fourth.

There was an element of luck in Lapize's middle victory, for Lucien Petit-Breton and Cyrille van Hauwaert were out in front with the victory seemingly between them, when a police horse unseated both of them. Like Lapize, Sellier might have won four. In 1921 a 15-man break was away when there was some confusion as to the route. The break took the right road and the chasers the wrong one. Despite having been led astray by the race director, the chasers had to retrace their path. Sellier was among them. He and one other set off after the break, catching it six hours later. But Sellier was too exhausted to take part in the final sprint.

For the next three years Sellier was on the right route, but his victories were not easy. In 1922 he survived an attack from a cloud of vicious insects, in 1923 he had to catch a break which had gained 15 minutes, and in 1924 he suffered two punctures within five miles just as the vital break was forming. Generally this classic became one for the sprinters because the distance discouraged adventurous breakaways. But Ernest Mottard escaped in 1930 with 180 miles left to ride and was not seen again until the finish.

Among the unlucky was Seamus Elliott in 1958. Sole attacker, he had a lead of more than a minute with three miles to go, when he smashed his

Though he had a very short pro career, Octave Lapize ranks among the top riders of all time. He won Paris-Brussels three years in a row from 1911–13, a feat matched by Felix Sellier 11 years later.

frame with his team car nowhere in sight. Grabbing a woman's bicycle, Elliott sprinted to the next corner where a touring cyclist offered him a better machine. By now the bunch was in sight and Elliott's hopes disintegrated.

One of the truly great victories occurred in 1966. Felice Gimondi, winner of the 1965 Tour, had won Paris-Roubaix seven days earlier, having attacked at a predetermined point. The following week at Paris-Brussels he was the favorite and a marked man for all, particularly Jacques Anquetil. None of this stopped Gimondi from breaking away and winning again, in record time.

Gimondi's record lasted nine years, but the race was not held for six of them. Traffic problems forced what, at the time, seemed a permanent cancellation. After the resumption of the event in 1973 Eddy Merckx and Marc de Meyer won narrow victories, and then came the fastest classic ever.

Belgium had had a disappointing year in 1975. Frenchman Bernard Thévenet caught and dropped Merckx to win the Tour and Dutchman Hennie Kuiper took the world championship in Belgium. Paris-Brussels was seen as a revenge match, but it was more.

Merckx was from Brussels and loved beating the Flemish riders in the Tour of Flanders. There was nothing that the Flemish riders would have loved more than to see Merckx's defeat in front of his own supporters. With a tailwind the pace was amazing. Twice Merckx, the only home rider in a bunch of Flemish, attacked on those rare hills that the route included. Twice he was pulled back. The final eight-man sprint was so furious that there was a gap of 19 seconds from first to eighth. André Dierickx led out, but was balked by a motorcycle marshal. Merckx swept past but Freddy Maertens was ready and took him comfortably. Maertens' average speed was 46.11 kph—28.65 mph over a course measuring just under 180 miles.

Maertens in his rainbow jersey was a hot favorite the following year, but Gimondi, uncharacteristically, was out for blood. With Francesco Moser the new national cycling hero, not a single Italian journalist had come to the event because Moser wasn't riding. While the Belgian sprinters watched each other, Gimondi attacked and was gone. Just as 10 years before, he was seen no more until the finish.

Recent editions have added little to Paris-Brussels' reputation. Long, and at times difficult, it is often ridden without conviction, particularly with Belgian cycling in the doldrums.

1932	Archambaud (F)
1933	Louviot (F)
1934	Magne (F)
1935	Magne (F)
1936	Magne (F)
1937	Cogan (F)
1938	Aimar Louis (F)
1939–40	not held
1941	Rossi (I) & Aimar Louis (F)
1942	Goasmat (F) & Idée (F)
1943	Somers (B)
1944	Carrara (I)
1945	Tassin (F)
1946	Coppi (I)
1947	Coppi (I)
1948	Berthon (F)
1949	Coste (F)
1950	Blomme (B)
1951	Koblet (Sw)
1952	Bobet (F)
1953	Anquetil (F)
1954	Anquetil (F)
1955	Anquetil (F)
1956	Anquetil (F)
1957	Anquetil (F)
1958	Anquetil (F)
1959	Moser, A. (I)
1960	Baldini (F)
1961	Anquetil (F)
1962	Bracke (B)
1963	Poulidor (F)
1964	Boucquet (B)
1965	Anquetil (F)
1966	Anquetil (F)
1967	Gimondi (I)
1968	Gimondi (I)
1969	van Springel (B)
1970	van Springel (B)
1971	Ocana (Sp)
1972	Swerts (B)

GRAND PRIX OF NATIONS

1973	Merckx (B)	1981	Gisiger (Sw)
1974	Schuiten (Nl)	1982	Hinault (F)
1975	Schuiten (Nl)	1983	Gisiger (Sw)
1976	Maertens (B)	1984	Hinault (F)
1977	Hinault (F)	1985	Mottet (F)
1978	Hinault (F)	1986	Kelly (Ir)
1979	Hinault (F)	1987	Mottet (F)
1980	van den Broucke (B)	1988	Mottet (F)

SPEED RECORD: Felice Gimondi, 45.311 kph in 1967
MOST VICTORIES: Jacques Anquetil, 9

Grand Prix of Nations

The only classic that is a time trial, the Grand Prix of Nations is also known as the Truth Race—a race in which a rider learns the truth about himself. But there is a much harder truth, which is that the race has never been popular with competitors except for those who relish the chance to ride alone.

The Nations' origin was in the French desire to copy the formula of the 1931 world championship and institute a revenge match. Once there were many time trials on the Continent, but spectators and riders generally preferred the more direct struggle of a conventional road race. Nevertheless, the race was promoted and has been run ever since, with comparatively few interruptions.

As with Bordeaux-Paris, distance and conditions have varied, so it is difficult to be precise about records. The original distance was 140 kilometers on a point-to-point course southwest of Paris. It included a fair number of hills, though none was particularly difficult for a fit roadman. Over the years the race was held in the same area, but shortened to 100 kilometers and then to 73 kilometers. Jacques Anquetil holds the record over the first two distances, and Felice Gimondi over the last. Gimondi also holds the overall record for the race.

In 1974 the Nations moved briefly to a 90 kilometer course at Angers, and then to Cannes and the Mediterranean hinterland, keeping the new distance. Roy Schuiten was the fastest winner on the Angers course, while Bernard Hinault set the record for the 89 kilometer Cannes course in the last of his five wins. In 1988 Charly Mottet set a record for the latest course—a course that appears to be established for many years to come. A good time trial course, such as the one near Cannes, is not just for the fast rider. It requires bike handling skill and the ability to climb well and descend well. Tight bends have to be expertly judged and sheer speed—though obviously desirable—will not produce a winner.

Anquetil is head and shoulders above all others in the Grand Prix with nine wins in nine rides, the first in 1953 when he was a teenager riding as an independent, or semi-professional. The closest finish was in 1959 when, with Anquetil sitting out the race, Roger Riviere was a firm favorite. But Aldo Moser, older brother of Francesco, was the victor by four seconds.

Many of the greats have won the race, among them Fausto Coppi, Louison Bobet, Anquetil, Eddy Merckx, and Bernard Hinault. Anquetil and Hinault were sometimes motivated by their quest for Pernod points, the Grand Prix being ridiculously overvalued in that competition.

Raymond Poulidor had a distinguished career, which spanned two decades. He rode the Tour de France 14 times from 1962–76, placing second three times and third five times. He's shown here in the Grand Prix of Nations, which he won in 1963.

Jacques Anquetil was one of the all-time greatest riders and, with nine victories, the undisputed champion of the Grand Prix of Nations. Here he's shown in the 1966 race, his final win.

1901	Fischer, J. (F)		
1902–05	not held		
1906	Petit-Breton (F)		
1907	Passerieu (F)		
1908	Beaugendre (F)		
1909	Faber (L)		
1910	Faber (L)		
1911	Lapize (F)		
1912	Heusghem (B)		
1913	Crupelandt (F)		
1914	Egg (Sw)		
1915–16	not held		
1917	Thijs (B)		
1918	Mantelet (F)		
1919	Thiberghien (B)		
1920	Christophe (F)		
1921	Pélissier, F. (F)		
1922	Pélissier, H. (F)		
1923	Deman (B)		
1924	Mottiat (B)		
1925	Verschueren (B)		

PARIS-TOURS

285 km

1926	Suter (Sw)	**1947**	Schotte (B)	**1968**	Reybrouck (B)
1927	Suter (Sw)	**1948**	Caput (F)	**1969**	van Springel (B)
1928	Verschueren (B)	**1949**	Ramon (F)	**1970**	Tschan (D)
1929	Frantz (L)	**1950**	Mahe (F)	**1971**	van Linden (B)
1930	Marechal (F)	**1951**	Dupont (F)	**1972**	van Tyghem (B)
1931	Leducq (F)	**1952**	Guegan (F)	**1973**	van Linden (B)
1932	Moineau (F)	**1953**	Schils (B)	**1974**	Moser, F. (I)
1933	Merviel (F)	**1954**	Scodeller (F)	**1975**	Maertens (B)
1934	Danneels (B)	**1955**	Dupont (F)	**1976**	de Witte (B)
1935	le Greves (F)	**1956**	Bouvet (F)	**1977**	Zoetemelk (Nl)
1936	Danneels (B)	**1957**	de Bruyne (B)	**1978**	Raas (Nl)
1937	Danneels (B)	**1958**	Desmet, G. (B)	**1979**	Zoetemelk (Nl)
1938	Rossi (I)	**1959**	van Looy (B)	**1980**	Willems (B)
1939	Bonduel (B)	**1960**	de Haan (Nl)	**1981**	Raas (Nl)
1940	not held	**1961**	Wouters (B)	**1982**	Vandenbroucke (B)
1941	Maye (F)	**1962**	de Roo (Nl)	**1983**	Peeters, L. (B)
1942	Maye (F)	**1963**	de Roo (Nl)	**1984**	Kelly (Ir)
1943	Gaudin (F)	**1964**	Reybrouck (B)	**1985**	Peeters, L. (B)
1944	Teisseire (F)	**1965**	Karstens (Nl)	**1986**	Anderson (A)
1945	Maye (F)	**1966**	Reybrouck (B)	**1987**	van der Poel (Nl)
1946	Schotte (B)	**1967**	van Looy (B)	**1988**	Pieters (Nl)

SPEED RECORD: Gerben Karstens, 45.029 kph in 1965
MOST VICTORIES: Gustaaf Danneels, Paul Maye, and Guido Reybrouck, 3 each

Paris-Tours

Paris-Tours lost its true character between 1974 and 1987 when the course was reversed, and then altered constantly. Although it would appear relatively flat on a small scale map, the traditional route was far from easy and produced a number of outstanding rides. The wind is inclined to be hostile and a number of short climbs towards the end add to the problems of tired riders. On the other hand, a following wind usually makes for a very fast pace.

Traffic problems in the early 1970s forced the organizers to find a new route, which has resulted in a number of variations. It was started from Tours and run to Versailles; it was started from Blois and run to Montlhéry; more recently it settled on a route from Blois (and then Créteil) to Chaville in the southwest suburbs of Paris. Sometimes it is known by the names of the start and finish towns, sometimes as the Grand Prix de l'Automne. For consistency, I shall stick to Paris-Tours.

Paris-Tours was first ridden in 1896 as an amateur race, financially supported by the newspaper *Paris-Vélo*, which offered generous prizes and certificates for all who finished within 18 hours. Professionals were allowed to ride the next edition, in 1901, and there was another 5-year gap before *L'Auto* took over the organization of the race in 1906.

After World War I, the race was lengthened slightly by adding a detour through Chinon and taking the approach to Tours over the hilly lanes on the southern banks of the Loire. Generally mild weather and favorable winds made for high speeds until 1921. It snowed. Almost half the field retired in Chartres while the Pélissier brothers forged ahead with Louis Mottiat and Albert de Jonghe. At Chateaudun conditions were too bad even for Henri Pélissier, the man of steel. Peeling off his cape, he handed it to his brother Francis, who wore two for the rest of the race. It is said that this transaction took place in a café over a glass of rum.

Meanwhile Eugène Christophe caught the leaders by a superhuman effort, typical of the man who thrived on adversity, and then went clear. Besieged by stops to repair bicycle or self, Pélissier chased and caught him three times, with Mottiat, the only other rider in the chase, struggling to hang on. Finally Pélissier got clear by several minutes, but then punctured. Hands frozen and unable to effect a repair, he tore off the damaged tire with his teeth. Riding on his rim, Pélissier caught Christophe once more, dropped him on the climb out of Azay-le-Rideau, and finished alone.

Unlike most classics, Paris-Tours had failed to produce a rider with sufficient mastery to stamp his name indelibly on the race until Gustave Danneels arrived in the 1930s. Danneels was the first to take the Ruban Jaune—an award long associated with this race. He won Paris-Brussels three times and, by one of those ironic twists of fate, his nephew, Guido Reybrouck, repeated the feat in the 1960s. The only other hat trick was Paul Maye's, but his wartime victories were achieved over fields of far inferior quality.

Paris-Tours became a battleground for the sprinters for many years. They dominated to such an extent that, in 1959, a three-lap circuit with the Alouette hill was added just before the finish. That year Claude Colette used the hill to break away on the first lap, but was joined by two Belgians. The second time over the hill one of the climbers broke away and went on to win alone. Had there been no hill he would very likely have won the bunch sprint anyhow, since he was none other than Rik van Looy.

One of the great champions of the 1960s was Jo de Roo, who was good enough to steal the Pernod title from Jacques Anquetil. Two years in succession de Roo did the Autumn double, winning Paris-Tours and the Tour of Lombardy on successive weekends. Rarely has anyone managed that even once because the two are so different in character.

Another innovation came in 1965 when derailleurs were banned. Riders used a single freewheel with a choice limited to two chainrings, with changes made by hand. Just like the Alouette hill, this ridiculous gear limit failed to make any significant difference to the outcome. Gerben Karstens won with the fastest speed ever, 45.029 kph, a record that stands to this day.

In 1968 van Looy became the only rider to win the eight races then considered orthodox classics with his victory in the Flèche Wallonne. Had Eddy Merckx known, later in 1968, what he was to learn subsequently, he might have ridden the last half-mile of Paris-Tours very differently. Reybrouck was seeking to emulate his uncle by winning three times. As they approached the line Merckx took charge, leading the sprint out of the final corner and in a position to win unchallenged. Then he suddenly pulled aside. Reybrouck came from the shelter of Merckx's wheel and held off the

Giuseppe Saronni leads Bernard Hinault in the 1979 Paris-Tours. The two thought the race was between them, but were surprised when Joop Zoetemelk (left) came up from behind with four miles to go and took the win.

desparate sprints of Walter Godefroot, Eric Leman and van Looy to complete his hat-trick. It was his reward for helping Merckx earlier in the season. Merckx never won Paris-Tours and Reybrouck retired in 1973 to open a car wash, calling his new business Paris-Tours, the same name which Danneels had given his garage.

The style of victory changed with the course in the 1960s and 1970s. The late attack became most popular, often coming in the last mile or two and frequently successful. Joop Zoetemelk was master of this tactic, as he demonstrated brilliantly in 1979. The previous year Bernard Hinault had seemed likely to win the Pernod Trophy, but had a disastrous finish in the Tour of Lombardy and lost the Pernod to Francesco Moser. In 1979 he was again leading the competition with Giuseppe Saronni the only other contender. The two joined forces in Paris-Tours to chase and catch a small break that had been away for some time. Unfortunately for them, they overlooked Zoetemelk, who came along when they caught the break. Their immediate task accomplished, Hinault and Saronni sat up for a breather. Zoetemelk went straight past with just four miles left and rode through the winding streets of Chaville to win by 40 seconds. Saronni took the bunch sprint with Hinault sixth.

Big-city courses like this one on the rue Rivoli in Paris are great for spectators, but can be impractical. Paris-Tours, for example, was rerouted several times due to traffic problems and now finishes in a Paris suburb.

It was at precisely the same point that Ludo Peeters, a very underrated rider, broke away in 1985 to take his second Paris-Tours in a competition that illustrated the value of team tactics. All eyes were on Adrie van der Poel, an outstanding finisher and Peeters' teammate. Van der Poel had won Paris-Brussels a few weeks before and was a marked man, especially for the 1984 winner Sean Kelly, who hadn't won a classic that season. Van der Poel attacked hard up the hill where Hinault, Saronni, and Zoetemelk had caught the break. Kelly, ever observant, pulled him back and, at that precise moment, Peeters surged out of the bunch to stay away and win.

Paris-Tours seems to have a secure future but should the finish move away from the twists and turns of Chaville there will be another new pattern to observe. What is certain, and has been proved conclusively through the various permutations of the race, is that no matter what tricks the organizers come up with, the smart riders will find ways of countering them.

1905	Gerbi (I)
1906	Brambilla (I)
1907	Garrigou (F)
1908	Faber (L)
1909	Cuniolo (I)
1910	Michelotto (I)
1911	Pélissier, H. (F)
1912	Oriani (I)
1913	Pélissier, H. (F)
1914	Bordin (I)
1915	Belloni (I)
1916	Torricelli (I)
1917	Thijs (B)
1918	Belloni (I)
1919	Girardengo (I)
1920	Pélissier, H. (F)
1921	Girardengo (I)
1922	Girardengo (I)
1923	Brunero (I)
1924	Brunero (I)
1925	Binda (I)
1926	Binda (I)
1927	Binda (I)
1928	Belloni (I)

TOUR OF LOMBARDY

260 km

ESINO LARIO
Varenna
Bellagio
Introbio
GHISALLO
Mandello
BALISIO
Erba
Lecco
S. Omobono
VALCAVA
VALPIANA
COMO
Brivio
Barzana
Merate
Usmate
Bergamo
Monza
MILAN

COMO
MILAN

1929	Fossati (I)	1950	Soldani (I)	1970	Bitossi (I)
1930	Mara (I)	1951	Bobet (F)	1971	Merckx (B)
1931	Binda (I)	1952	Minardi (I)	1972	Merckx (B)
1932	Negrini (I)	1953	Landi (I)	1973	Gimondi (I)
1933	Piemontesi (I)	1954	Coppi (I)	1974	de Vlaeminck (B)
1934	Guerra (I)	1955	Maule (I)	1975	Moser (I)
1935	Mollo (I)	1956	Darrigade (F)	1976	de Vlaeminck (B)
1936	Bartali (I)	1957	Ronchini (I)	1977	Baronchelli (I)
1937	Bini (I)	1958	Defilippis (I)	1978	Moser (I)
1938	Cinelli (I)	1959	van Looy (B)	1979	Hinault (F)
1939	Bartali (I)	1960	Daems (B)	1980	de Wolf, A. (B)
1940	Bartali (I)	1961	Taccone (I)	1981	Kuiper (Nl)
1941	Ricci (I)	1962	de Roo (Nl)	1982	Saronni (I)
1942	Bini (I)	1963	de Roo (Nl)	1983	Kelly (Ir)
1943-44	not held	1964	Motta (I)	1984	Hinault (F)
1945	Ricci (I)	1965	Simpson (GB)	1985	Kelly (Ir)
1946	Coppi (I)	1966	Gimondi (I)	1986	Baronchelli (I)
1947	Coppi (I)	1967	Bitossi (I)	1987	Argentin (I)
1948	Coppi (I)	1968	van Springel (B)	1988	Mottet (F)
1949	Coppi (I)	1969	Monsere (B)		

SPEED RECORD: Sean Kelly, 41.208 kph in 1985
MOST VICTORIES: Fausto Coppi, 5

Tour of Lombardy

As Milan-San Remo, opening the classic season, is known as the Primrose, so the season-closing Tour of Lombardy, in Italy, is known as the Race of the Falling Leaves. On its famous hilly route to Como it is a fine spectacle, but this is another race that has had difficulties.

For many years it ended on the famous Vigorelli track in Milan. In 1961 the organizer, Signor Torriani, designed a completely new route that started in Milan, moved north to Lake Como, then followed the general outline of the lake but with several steep passes thrown in. The climbs were not particularly long, but there were enough—with grades up to 20%—to keep the sprinters from winning quite as easily. In 1985 the course reverted to a Milan finish almost 50 miles from the final climb, but fortunately this was only a temporary state of affairs with the race returning to its Como finish in 1988.

The Tour of Lombardy is the oldest of the great Italian races, going back to 1905 when it was held on a cold and very foggy day in November over a course of roads and mule tracks no more than 16 inches wide. Giovanni Gerbi won by more than 40 minutes—impressive sounding, but in reality far from it.

There was a railroad crossing 20 miles from the start. Gerbi had decided to make his first attack here, and was accompanied by an Italian and two French riders. As Gerbi rushed towards the crossing a spectator threw a bicycle into the middle of the road, felling the two Frenchmen. Gerbi rode on happily and the crossing gate closed. Eight minutes passed before Lucien Petit-Breton, leading the next group, was allowed through. Then came a forest of tacks, on which Gustave Garrigou punctured twice. Gerbi was a quarter of an hour up, having tripled his lead within 60 miles of the start. But Garrigou chased determinedly, reducing the deficit to four minutes, when carloads of Italian supporters suddenly arrived and sprin-

119

kled the road with another helping of tacks. Meanwhile Gerbi was being paced up front by a number of touring cyclists who just happened to be on the road.

The Italian officials had done what they could to control the event, but were powerless against the hundreds of *tifosi*. Even today these zealous fans represent a considerable threat, although the objects of their idolatry are likely to suffer under the strict rules of the Union Cycliste Internationale. Once it was normal for an Italian rider to be pushed up hills. Now a helping hand is almost certain to incur heavy penalties.

It looked as though Gerbi's excesses would ruin the Tour of Lombardy, because few foreigners were willing to travel all the way to Italy to suffer as Garrigou had. But, happily, things were put right.

In 1920 Henri Pélissier became the first triple winner, although it was only by chance that he rode at all in 1911. Petit-Breton had met him at a railway station in Paris and had talked so enthusiastically about going for a week's racing in Italy that Pélissier rushed home to pack his bags and go too. He was on the train within six hours of the chance meeting. Ten days later he won the Tour of Lombardy. His second win came two years later.

Pélissier's record was short-lived, with Costante Girardengo taking a third win in 1922—a time when foreign riders were rarely seen in Lombardy—and Alfredo Binda completing his hat trick a mere five years later.

It wasn't until after World War II that foreigners returned to Lombardy in large numbers and then it was to find Fausto Coppi at his most unbeatable. Winner five times—four in successive years—Coppi always attacked on the Madonna del Ghisallo, then a narrow, unpaved road. In only one of his five successful years was Coppi not first to the top of the dreaded climb, and that one time he won in a sprint finish.

For 30 years no Frenchman finished in the top three, in part because relatively few rode the race. In 1951 Louison Bobet won Milan-San Remo and went to Milan with hopes for an Italian double. For once Coppi was not first up the Ghisallo. Instead, Giancarlo Astrua led him and Bobet by about a minute. On the descent eight regrouped and Bobet won the sprint after being last at the entry to the track.

Two years later the Ghisallo was paved, making it an easier climb by far. Sprint finishes of more than eight riders became so common for a while that the organizers had to think of ways to invigorate the Lombardy tour, which ended back in Milan, too far from the hills for any final selection to be made. Rik van Looy's 1959 win was from an 85-man sprint—a fine spectacle no doubt, but an indictment of what had for many years been one of the toughest events on the calendar.

The attempted solution was the addition of the Wall of Sormano, a path about two yards wide and so steep that Jacques Anquetil decided on a gear of 42 x 27. But this innovation failed, since most of the field rode up like touring cyclists, or walked. In 1961 Imerio Massignan rode the whole way and was rejoined on the other side by Vito Taccone. Claiming that the climb had finished him, Taccone persuaded Massignan to tow him to the new finish in Como, on condition that Taccone would not contest the sprint. As they neared the finish Taccone mysteriously rediscovered his strength, leaving Massignan several yards behind at the line.

The course that became known as the classic route didn't stop Jo de Roo from winning, but it did help to create two of the finest battles in the history of the Lombardy tour.

In 1964 Tom Simpson opened the hostilities early. Gianni Motta saw the danger and drew level with Simpson, bringing a handful of others. Simpson and Motta attacked one another mercilessly over the passes until

The cobbled climbs of the Tour of Lombardy are wider but no less strenuous than those of the spring classics. Briton Tom Simpson, at front in the world champion's rainbow jersey, rode to victory in the 1965 race.

Simpson had to yield and watch Motta ride away to a fine solo victory. The next year Simpson was world champion and was determinied to justify his rainbow jersey. On the Ghisallo—a long way from Como—Simpson shook off all challengers except one, Motta. Again it was a duel with no quarter but this time Simpson was stronger. At Argegno, with two climbs to come, he finally forced Motta to yield and went on to reverse the outcome of the previous year. The Continental press wrote that no rider in the world could have stayed with Simpson that day.

Another meritorious winner was Franco Bitossi, the Italian with a heart complaint. In front in 1970 with Felice Gimondi and Raymond Poulidor, Bitossi found that his legs were willing but his heart was not. Forced to stop and rest, Bitossi watched his rivals ride away. After recuperating he caught the two, dropped them, and won alone.

Oddly, Eddy Merckx didn't star in the Tour of Lombardy as often as one might expect. He won in 1970 and 1971, but was disqualified the next year, though he arrived in Como four minutes clear of the second finisher, Gimondi. Merckx's urine test was positive, but Merckx was not the only one to point out that he had won 445 races as a pro and had only twice failed the dope test, both times in Italy.

Of course Bernard Hinault wanted to do as well as Merckx, but Hinault had to wait for the honor. In 1978 he arrived at the start leading the Pernod competition by 275 points to Francesco Moser's 263. The Tour of Lombardy offered 60, 40, and 30 points to the first three, so Hinault needed to stop Moser from winning. And if Moser finished second, Hinault had to be third.

Rarely could Hinault have ridden worse. Instead of using his superior climbing power, he followed Moser everywhere. Falling twice on the Schignano—which he blamed on the *tifosi*—Hinault had to struggle to catch up. The 1,302-foot San Fermo della Battaglia provided him a last chance to attack, but he held back. A nine-man group approached Como for the sprint that would very likely decide both the race and the Pernod.

Inexplicably, Hinault picked Joop Zoetemelk's wheel to follow. As Bernt Johanssen initiated the sprint with Wladimiro Panizza on his wheel and Moser next, Hinault was already badly placed. When Panizza faded, Moser swung round, took Johanssen a hundred yards from the line, and won comfortably. Hinault, realizing his mistake too late, had enough power to take a useless third. Blaming every Italian rider in the break for his misjudgment, Hinault swore revenge.

The following year Hinault had already assured himself of the Pernod victory when he returned to the Tour of Lombardy. Attacking early in the race on the Balisio he shattered the field and only six stuck with him over the top. On the Intelvi he attacked again and this time only Silvano Contini could hold the pace. Hinault didn't attack again since he knew he could outsprint Contini, and he did.

The dominant classics rider of the mid 1980s, Sean Kelly, took his first classic victory in 1983. He won the Tour of Lombardy by a tire's width from Greg LeMond and Adrie van der Poel—one of the closest sprint finishes ever in this event.

In 1984 Hinault allowed an early break to gain a fair lead and took the bunch back up to it. Then, as if he were a cat toying with two mice, Hinault watched Charly Mottet and Stephen Roche ride away on the Schignano. Two others were allowed to chase. When the motorcycle marshals announced that Mottet and Roche had a one-minute lead, Hinault struck. With a few hopefuls clinging to his wheel in the hope that he would burn himself out, Hinault caught the chasers in less than two miles. At the foot of the last climb he caught Mottet and Roche. On the climb Tommy Prim attacked, apparently another signal. Immediately Hinault was past him and away, reaching Como with just under a minute to spare. He never did it the easy way if there was a hard way to be found.

Sean Kelly sprinted to victory in 1985, the first year the route was reversed. The following year Gianbattista Baronchelli won with a late attack while Kelly watched him with that characteristic caution that has cost the Irishman many a race. In 1987 the French Systeme-U team should have sewn it up long before the finish. They had three riders in a 10-man break, but messed it up, allowing Moreno Argentin back in after he had been dropped and then failing to agree on any battle plan. Eric Boyer tried to escape in the closing miles, but Argentin was ready for him and took the sprint comfortably in a Tour of Lombardy that seemed a long way removed from the glories of Pélissier and Coppi, Merckx and Hinault.

WINNERS OF THE DESGRANGE-COLOMBO CHALLENGE

1948	Schotte (B)	**1952**	Kubler (Sw)	**1956**	de Bruyne (B)
1949	Coppi (I)	**1953**	Petrucci (I)	**1957**	de Bruyne (B)
1950	Kubler (Sw)	**1954**	Kubler (Sw)	**1958**	de Bruyne (B)
1951	Bobet (F)	**1955**	Ockers (B)		

TOP THREE FOR THE SUPER PRESTIGE PERNOD TROPHY

Year	First	Pts	Second	Pts	Third	Pts
1958	Forestier (F)					
1959	Anglade (F)	165	Riviere (F)	150	Fore (B) & van Looy (B)	115
1960	Graczyk (F)	160	Cerami (B)	141	Nancini (I)	132
1961	Anquetil (F)	241	Poulidor (F)	198	van Looy (B)	197
1962	de Roo (Nl)	170	Planckaert, J. (B)	148	Daems (B)	120
1963	Anquetil (F)	260	Simpson (GB)	195	Poulidor (F)	180
1964	Poulidor (F)	230	Janssen (Nl)	197	Anquetil (F)	165
1965	Anquetil (F)	216	Simpson (GB)	185	Sels (B)	170
1966	Anquetil (F)	235	Gimondi (I)	224	Poulidor (F)	213
1967	Janssen (Nl)	284	Merckx (B)	231	Gimondi (I)	225
1968	van Springel (B)	194	Gimondi (I)	180	Godefroot (B)	165
1969	Merckx (B)	412	Gimondi (I)	219	van Springel (B)	203
1970	Merckx (B)	409	van Springel (B)	190	Ocana (Sp)	178
1971	Merckx (B)	570	Ocana (Sp)	150	Zoetemelk (Nl) & Petterson (Sd)	140
1972	Merckx (B)	438	Poulidor (F)	210	Guimard (F)	148
1973	Merckx (B)	465	Ocana (Sp)	310	Zoetemelk (Nl)	190
1974	Merckx (B)	455	de Vlaeminck (B)	205	Verbeeck (B)	159
1975	Merckx (B)	415	de Vlaeminck (B)	266	Moser (I)	255
1976	Maertens (B)	332	Moser (I)	175	Zoetemelk (Nl)	170
1977	Maertens (B)	236	de Vlaeminck (B)	213	Hinault (F)	190
1978	Moser (I)	323	Hinault (F)	305	Zoetemelk (Nl)	184
1979	Hinault (F)	421	Saronni (I)	330	Zoetemelk (Nl)	325
1980	Hinault (F)	315	de Wolf, A. (B)	218	Moser (I)	210
1981	Hinault (F)	325	de Vlaeminck (B)	185	Raas (Nl)	155
1982	Hinault (F)	266	Saronni (I)	250	Contini (I)	123
1983	LeMond (US)	245	Kelly (Ir)	220	Saronni (I) & Raas (Nl)	175
1984	Kelly (Ir)	450	Hinault (F)	305	Anderson (A)	197
1985	Kelly (Ir)	309	Anderson (A)	288	LeMond (US)	208
1986	Kelly (Ir)	910	LeMond (US)	660	Criquielion (B)	505
1987	Roche (Ir)	800	Kelly (Ir)	560	Criquielion (B)	490

Super Prestige Pernod Trophy

Established in 1948 in memory of Henri Desgrange and Emilio Colombo (editor of the *Gazzetta dello Sport*), the Desgrange-Colombo Challenge was a competition that awarded points for finishing positions in designated races. There was always disagreement over which races to include, but the successful rider each year was still accorded considerable prestige and a substantial cash prize. By the late 1950s it was obvious that the disagreement was becoming so serious that the Challenge would not last long.

A new competition sponsored by the Pernod organization—makers of a liqueur—began in 1958. At first open only to Frenchmen, in 1959 and 1960 it was accessible to any pro, but judged exclusively on the basis of French events. In 1961 the Pernod competition was completely remodeled to include most of the top European races, and since then it has been accepted as an unofficial, season-long professional points championship.

The first three Pernod Super Prestige Trophies went to Jean Forestier, Henri Anglade, and Jean Graczyk—Frenchmen all. When the competition went international in 1961 the qualifying events and point scales were very different from those in use in 1987. Over the years races were added. The number of points attributed to each race was increased and points were awarded for lower finishing positions.

Accepting that the Pernod Trophy did its job—to measure the outstanding pro roadman of each season—it nevertheless had numerous faults.

First, too many races were included—33 in 1987.

Second, some of these were palpably unsuitable, such as the Tour de l'Avenir, created for young professionals and rarely ridden by established stars. Others, the San Sebastian Classic among them, had neither the status nor the field to justify inclusion.

Third, several races overlapped, not only as described earlier with the Tour of Spain often clashing with the late spring classics, but with minor stage races being run simultaneously, such as Paris-Nice and Tirreno-Adriatico, both of which have been qualifiers for many years.

Fourth, there was a heavy bias towards minor stage races held in France, with the Dauphiné Libéré and the Midi-Libre both included, for example.

Finally, and perhaps the strongest criticism—the points awarded for places were insufficiently generous to the winner. The 1987 Tour de France was worth 180, 155, 135, 120, 110, 100, 90, 85, 80, 75, 70, 65, 60, 55, and 50 points for riders in the top 15 positions. In other words, the rider finishing seventh in the Tour received half the points given to the winner—in this case Laurent Fignon and Stephen Roche respectively. Fignon received as many points for finishing seventh in the Tour as did Moreno Argentin for winning Liège-Bastogne-Liège or the Tour of Lombardy.

Despite these criticisms, the winner of the Pernod was generally recognized as the best pro roadman of the year and the list of winners shows that top riders almost always filled the lead positions.

It isn't valid to compare riders from year to year based on their Pernod points because the total number of points available changed frequently. In a 1986 *Cycling Weekly* article I wrote that it might be informative to calculate the number of points gained by the Pernod Trophy winner as a percentage of the total points won by the top five riders in the competition. Ranking by this method is:

% of total points available	Rider(s) who achieved % of total and year(s) that they did	
51%	Merckx (B)	1971
42%	Merckx (B)	1972
41%	Merckx (B)	1974
40%	Merckx (B)	1970
35%	Merckx (B)	1969 and 1973
34%	Maertens (B)	1976
	Hinault (F)	1981
33%	Kelly (Ir)	1984
30%	Merckx (B)	1975
	Hinault (F)	1980 and 1982
	Kelly (Ir)	1986
29%	Anquetil (F)	1963
	Janssen (Nl)	1967
	Moser (I)	1978
	Roche (Ir)	1987

Eddy Merckx's long domination of the sport is clear. Twice he took 35% of the points won by the top five—the only one to do so well. On three other occasions he climbed to 40%, and in 1971 reached an impressive 51%.

1987 was the last year for the Super Prestige Trophy and other competitions sponsored by Pernod, due to a French government ban on the advertising of alcohol in sports promotions. If the ban is permanent, the Pernod Trophy will no doubt eventually be replaced by some other competition, just as Pernod itself replaced the Desgrange-Colombo Challenge.

Others may not agree with my criticisms of the Pernod series, and the Pernod company can't be praised enough for all that it has done for cycling—and several other sports. But I hope that any similar competition will be limited to something like the 20 events described in this book. Also, I hope the points scale will be adjusted so that the second place rider in any race never receives more than half the points awarded to the winner. And if minor places in stage races are to count, recognition should be made of the King of the Mountains and the points winner. Whom do you consider to be the more meritorious riders in the 1987 Tour—Luis Herrera and Jean-Paul van Poppel (KOM and points winners) or Gerhard Zadrobilek and Luciano Loro (14th and 15th places)?

Of course cycling must and will continue to evolve. If the new races such as the United States-based Coors Classic or the Clasico R.C.N. held in Colombia come to have the international reputations that the top 20—or most of them—now enjoy, then these should be included in any future overall competition.

Almost anything will be better than the points classification of the Federation Internationale de Cyclisme Professional, the world governing body of pro cycling. Based on performances over the most recent three years, the FICP-*Vélo* standings at the end of 1987 had Sean Kelly heading the classification, despite being completely overshadowed that year by his fellow Irishman, Stephen Roche.

There was no international season-long competition in 1988, but the Perrier company has agreed to sponsor a World Cup for individual riders and trade teams for three years, 1989–91. The top three positions of individuals in 1988, according to the Perrier calculations would have been Steven Rooks, Kelly, and Adrie van der Poel. If the Pernod competition had happened, the top three would have been Rooks, Kelly, and Charly Mottet. One of the main differences between the two systems is that stage races are not included in the Perrier competition. This, and other faults of the World Cup are addressed in the envoy.

Ruban Jaune

The idea of a yellow ribbon for record speed in cycling was no doubt copied from the speed record for Atlantic crossing by ships. The conditions for awarding the record are very strict. The speed must be made in a race or stage of at least 200 kilometers with the distance accurately measured. The time must be certified by two timekeepers independently, using certified equipment that has been recently calibrated. In the last 20 years there has been also an unofficial agreement that only in accepted classics would speeds be considered to have met these conditions.

Because of these demanding conditions the record very rarely changes hands. There are races in which speeds high enough to be worth checking against the record are very unlikely. For example, the Ardennes classics, where difficult terrain and unusual winds combine to keep speeds low.

Gus Danneels was first to be credited with the official record with his 41.455 kph victory in Paris-Tours in 1936. Jules Rossi raised it in the same race two years later and, with World War II intervening, it was 10 years before Rik van Steenbergen set a new record in Paris-Roubaix. In 1955 Jacques Dupont restored the record to Paris-Tours. After this the arguments began.

Jean Anastasi won the St. Etienne-Avignon stage of Paris-Nice in 1961 at 44.917 kph and was declared the new record holder, despite criticisms that the stage had not been properly measured. Jo de Roo had some claim to the title with his 44.903 kph win in Paris-Tours in 1962, but Walter Martin had won the 1961 Milan-Turin at an average speed of 45.094 kph. Marino Vigna won the Three Varesine Valleys race in 1964 at 47.17 kph. Walter Godefroot scored a stage win in the 1964 Tour of Tunisia at 53.349 kph, but over a distance of only 150 kilometers.

The arguments were settled to the satisfaction of most, though not the individual riders who claimed the record, when Peter Post recorded 45.129

kph to win Paris-Roubaix in 1964. That record stood for more than a decade until Freddy Maertens' success in Paris-Brussels in 1975 at 46.11 kph.

There has been no increase since and the arguments have abated. Post's record deserves special mention, for to win Paris-Roubaix at that speed despite the difficult cobbles to be negotiated is quite exceptional.

Maertens' record also ended a minor controversy surrounding Roger Kindt, who won the 1969 Milan to Vignola at 45.995 kph—faster than Post but slower than Maertens. At first, Kindt's speed seemed likely to be ratified, but a mystery surrounding the post-race medical control was never cleared up.

The progression of the record, as far as I can establish it, follows. Those claims which reached a sufficient speed but were never ratified are in italic.

RUBAN JAUNE WINNERS

Year	Rider	Race	kph	mph
1936	Danneels (B)	Paris-Tours	41.455	25.759
1938	Rossi (I)	Paris-Tours	42.097	26.158
1948	van Steenbergen (B)	Paris-Roubaix	43.612	27.099
1955	Dupont (F)	Paris-Tours	43.766	27.195
1961	Anastasi (F)	St. Etienne-Avignon	44.917	27.91
1961	*Martin (I)*	*Milan-Turin*	*45.094*	*28.022*
1962	*de Roo (Nl)*	*Paris-Tours*	*44.903*	*27.901*
1964	*Vigna (I)*	*Three Varesine Valleys*	*47.17*	*29.311*
1964	Post (Nl)	Paris-Roubaix	45.129	28.042
1969	*Kindt (B)**	*Milan-Vignola*	*45.995*	*28.58*
1975	Maertens (B)	Paris-Brussels	46.11	28.651

* Some records show Attilo Rota (I) as the winner, with Kindt disqualified.

World Hour Record

No cycling record receives as much publicity or claims as much attention as the world hour record. The record is held by the rider who has covered the longest distance in an hour. Attempts are held on a track because numerous variables could affect the outcome if on the road, yet most riders who have held the record have been primarily roadmen.

In theory there are several hour records—amateur and professional, on covered and open tracks, at sea level and above but, as far as I am concerned, such subdivisions are spurious. When Carl Lewis took the 100-meter record from Calvin Smith in 1987, nobody raised questions about where the record was established, on what kind of track or by a runner of what status.

The first official hour record was 35.325 kilometers, set in 1893 by Henri Desgrange. Within five years it had been raised by more than 5 kilometers. Over the next 40 years there were 12 successful attempts, but only a bit more than 5 kilometers was added to the distance during that period.

Interest in the record tended to run in phases. After the initial flurry there was a lull until Lucien Petit-Breton came along in 1905, to be followed by a period of intense competition between Marcel Berthet and Oscar Egg. Then 19 years passed before the record was improved, but Maurice Richard's success was the signal for a fresh outbreak of attempts that ended with Fausto Coppi's record in 1942. Another 14 years elapsed before Jacques Anquetil succeeded in bettering Coppi and interest swelled again. Four successful rides were registered in three years before another gap, this time of nine years.

After Anquetil's 1967 record failed ratification—because he refused to submit to medical control—interest was reawakened, with titles take by Ferdi Bracke in 1967, Ole Ritter in 1968, and, inevitably, Eddy Merckx in 1972. Merckx's record, like Coppi's, was considered unbeatable in the foreseeable future, not because of the distance but because of the record holder. There was some justification for this—Coppi held the record for 14 years and Merckx for 12. Francesco Moser not only improved on Merckx, but did so twice in five days. His first win, by 1,377 meters, was the biggest margin since 1898. His second set the record that stands—51.151 kilometers.

There have been other claims. In 1913 Richard Weise covered 42.276 kilometers compared to Egg's then-current record of 42.122. Egg immediately lodged an objection. He did not challenge Weise's distance, but argued that the Buffalo track in Paris had been measured incorrectly when Egg set his record in 1912. When the track was remeasured, it was found that the distance was 301.7 meters instead of the 300 previously supposed. This raised Egg's record to 42.36 kilometers—more than covered by Weise in Berlin.

Oscar Egg, left, set the world hour record three times—in 1912, 1913, and 1914. The Swiss rider was an exceptional all-rounder. This is a copy of a souvenir photo which Egg inscribed to a fan in 1919. Francesco Moser (right) holds the current hour record of 51.151 km set in Mexico in 1984. Although the Italian's unconventional aerodynamic equipment caused an uproar, his record was accepted by the Union Cycliste Internationale.

There was controversy again in 1933. This time Jan van Hout covered 44.588 kilometers on a Dutch track and Egg objected to the distance claimed. The Roermond track was remeasured and the distance reduced. But this time a counterclaim was lodged and further measurement confirmed van Hout's original distance. By then Maurice Richard had beaten both Egg and van Hout, making the dispute academic.

Who was the greatest hour record holder? It is difficult to compare riders of different generations. One possible method is to examine the best seasons of each and determine how many of the top races each won at what may be taken as the peak of his career. This measurement has some relevance to the world hour record.

Though Coppi's ride added only 31 meters to the record distance—the smallest improvement ever—his record was hailed as unbeatable because it was Coppi. In 1942, with racing severely curtailed by the war, Coppi had taken the Italian road championship and had enjoyed a fairly full season in Italy, without winning any other of the more important races. There is no apparent reason why he should not have been fully fresh when he reported to the Vigorelli track on November 7 for his successful attempt.

Merckx's 50 road wins in 1972 included Milan-San Remo, Ghent-Wevelgem, Liège-Bastogne-Liège, the Flèche Wallonne, the Tour of Italy, the Tour de France, and the Tour of Lombardy. No one else, incidentally, has ever won five classics and two major stage races in a season. Before the end of October Merckx was in Mexico City to add 778 meters to the record—the biggest increase since Egg in 1913.

Coppi was not well known when he took the hour record. Anquetil was near the beginning of his pro career, Ercole Baldini was still an amateur, Roger Rivière had never won a major race, and neither Bracke nor Ritter was putting an illustrious career at risk. Merckx, on the other hand, completed the most successful road season in cycling history and three weeks later became the rider to cover the most distance in an hour.

Physiological tests conducted at the Milan Institute helped explain Merckx's success. He had the body structure to be a better climber than Coppi or Louison Bobet, legs that allowed him to take on the best road sprinters in the world, and a pulse rate so slow that he recovered faster than any other cyclist recorded except Gino Bartali.

Merckx, who was obsessed by detail, designed his own track frame for the record attempt. But he was overshadowed by Moser's, which had a sloping top tube, lenticular wheels of different sizes and upturned bars. For awhile it seemed that the Union Cycliste Internationale might refuse to ratify Moser's record, ridiculous though it seems now that such bikes are common.

WORLD HOUR RECORD

Year	Rider	Track	Gear	Km	Gain	Miles
1893	Desgrange (F)	Paris, Buffalo	unknown	35.325		21.950
1894	Dubois (F)	Paris, Buffalo	unknown	38.220	2895	23.747
1897	van den Eynde (B)	Paris, Vincennes	unknown	39.240·	1020	24.383
1898	Hamilton (US)	Denver, Colorado	unknown	40.781	1541	25.340
1905	Petit-Breton (F)	Paris, Buffalo	unknown	41.110	329	25.545
1907	Berthet (F)	Paris, Buffalo	unknown	41.520	410	25.799
1912	Egg (Sw)	Paris, Buffalo	unknown	42.360	840	26.321
1913	Berthet (F)	Paris, Buffalo	unknown	42.741	381	26.558
1913	Egg (Sw)	Paris, Buffalo	unknown	43.525	784	27.045
1913	Berthet (F)	Paris, Buffalo	unknown	43.775	250	27.200
1914	Egg (Sw)	Paris, Buffalo	unknown	44.247	472	27.494
1933	Richard (F)	St. Trond, Belgium	24 X 7	44.777	530	27.823
1935	Olmo (I)	Milan, Vigorelli	24 X 7	45.090	313	28.012
1936	Richard (F)	Milan, Vigorelli	24 X 7	45.398	308	28.209
1937	Slaats (Nl)	Milan, Vigorelli	24 X 7	45.558	160	28.308
1937	Archambaud (F)	Milan, Vigorelli	24 X 7	45.840	282	28.484
1942	Coppi (I)	Milan, Vigorelli	52 X 15	45.871	31	28.503
1956	Anquetil (F)	Milan, Vigorelli	52 X 15	46.159	288	28.682
1956	Baldini (I)	Milan, Vigorelli	52 X 15	46.393	234	28.827
1957	Rivière (F)	Milan, Vigorelli	52 X 15	46.923	530	29.157
1958	Rivière (F)	Milan, Vigorelli	53 X 15	47.346	423	29.419
1967	Bracke (B)	Rome, Olympic	53 X 15	48.093	747	29.884
1968	Ritter (D)	Mexico, Olympic	54 X 15	48.653	560	30.232
1972	Merckx (B)	Mexico, Olympic	52 X 14	49.431	778	39.715
1984	Moser (I)	Mexico, Municipal	56 X 15	50.808	1377	31.571
1984	Moser (I)	Mexico, Municipal	57 X 15	51.151	343	31.784

Moser's fastest kilometer in Mexico was 1:08.358. While seconds slower than world championship times, it is still fast for a man intending to cover 50 kilometers instead of just one. His second successful ride saw him cover the first five kilometers from a standing start in 5:47.16—a time beaten by only five riders in the qualifying round of the 1987 world pursuit championship. While they faced only four rides over two days, Moser kept this speed up for 10 successive stretches of 5 kilometers in the one ride.

His 1983 season had been far from successful. At 32 he might have thought that his best years were behind him—after all, winning Paris-Roubaix three years in a row is extraordinary, and few have been world champion on both road and track. But Moser is a far from ordinary champion. Like Merckx he paid great attention to detail. Unlike Merckx, he made his attempts in January, almost three months after the end of the road season. Moser's unconventional training—fast roadwork including uphill sprints—hardly seemed appropriate for what is essentially a marathon pursuit. But it was in his equipment that Moser made the greatest innovations.

Moser's one-piece, ankle-length suit was contrary to Union Cycliste Internationale regulations, as was his bicycle in more ways than one. There was argument afterwards about the disk wheels, but the clearest infringement of rules was over a detail—the bottom bracket was not centered at a point between 24 and 30 centimeters from the ground. Does it matter? Obviously not. Moser powered a two-wheeled bicycle further in an hour than anyone and that should be all that matters. He passed medical control on both occasions and the Union Cycliste Internationale officials present for both attempts did not suggest that his bicycle or clothing might risk disqualification. Through Moser's incredible ride, cycling technology took several major steps forwards.

Envoy

"Time present and time past
Are both perhaps present in time future
And time future contained in time past."

So wrote T. S. Eliot in the *Four Quartets*. One of the greatest problems for the writer of any historical review is knowing when to stop, because history itself does not stop. Since this book is a history of the major races for professional cyclists, it too has no natural place to stop.

For 30 years the Pernod competitions gave a crude but adequate guide to the top races in Europe. Now they have been replaced by an entirely new competition, the Perrier World Cup. The points scale for the 1989 Perrier competition follows.

Points awarded to top 10 finishers (1st, 2nd, 3rd, ...)	Race
12, 9, 8, 7, 6, 5, 4, 3, 2, 1	Milan-San Remo
	Tour of Flanders
	Paris-Roubaix
	Liège-Bastogne-Liège
	Amstel Gold Race
14, 11, 10, 9, 8, 7, 6, 5, 4, 3	Wincanton Classic
	Grand Prix of the Americas
	San Sebastian-San Sebastian
	Championship of Zürich
16, 13, 12, 11, 10, 9, 8, 7, 6, 5	Grand Prix Liberation (team points only)
	Paris-Tours
	Tour of Lombardy

Though the Perrier company is to be thanked and congratulated for sponsoring this new competition, there are some criticisms that can be fairly made. Although it would apparently have produced the right winner

137

in 1988, a competition that replaces races like the Tour de France and the world championship with new races such as the Wincanton Classic is open to question. It seems unfair, too, that 160 of the 200 places available in each event are open only to riders in the top 20 teams according to the three-year FICP-*Vélo* ranking. And increasing the point value of races as the season wears on is bizarre. No rider would really prefer victory in Paris-Tours to victory in Paris-Roubaix, except in order to improve his chances in an artificial competition.

But it is important to have targets and the Perrier company has provided a target that will maintain the enthusiasm of the riders. I opened this book by quoting Bernard Levin. I close it by quoting Ralph Waldo Emerson: "Nothing great was ever achieved without enthusiasm."

Appendix 1

The Riders

Comparing sports stars from different generations is never easy, yet never ceases to attract archivists, writers, and general enthusiasts. How did Rocky Marciano compare with Joe Louis, Muhammad Ali with Marciano, Holmes with Ali? How will Mike Tyson eventually measure up against all of them, not to mention the heroes from before World War II like Jack Dempsey and Gene Tunney?

If there is no easy answer, there are one or two things that may be safely said. Many people are nostalgic about sportsmen who made the headlines during a particular time. Those who, as teenagers or young adults, watched Joe Louis may well be unshaken in their conviction that he was the greatest. Secondly, so many things have improved in the last 30 years—diet, training, equipment, technique—that most modern performers can compete at levels that were once open only to the very greatest champions. But comparisons tend to be made emotionally rather than logically, which isn't bad, for it would be a sad world where logic always triumphed.

In cycling, comparisons are complicated by the creation of new races and the occasional demise of old ones. The only fair method is to try to assess performers against their peers. Thus it may be judged that, for example, Octave Lapize was unequalled for a very short period, Henri Pélissier was the rider feared by all immediately after World War I, Fausto Coppi was regarded as the *campionissimo* immediately after World War II, Louison Bobet was the dominant rider of the mid 1950s, and so on. Nevertheless, it is still not easy to compare Lapize with Pélissier or with Coppi.

Another sort of claim is often made. Those who consider Marciano better than Ali would be quick to argue that the latter had no real competition—he looked good and had an impressive string of victories, but the boxers whom he beat were mostly no-hopers. Not true, but it's hard to counter. The fact is, most great champions make the opposition look ordinary.

For years there were many who claimed that Coppi would have ridden Merckx into the ground. They'd argue that Coppi had to contend with Gino Bartali, Rik van Steenbergen, Ferdi Kubler, Hugo Koblet, Bobet, and a host of others. But the evidence that Merckx similarly had to contend with Felice Gimondi, Joop Zoetemelk, Jan Janssen, Roger de Vlaeminck, Jan Raas and so on was quickly discounted.

Despite these difficulties I have attempted to compare the riders of the last 90 years using two measurements.

The first method allocates points to the top 20 races as I place them in order of merit. Some will disagree with the values assigned (shown in Table 1), but any argument has its counterclaim. The points are consistent throughout the history of a race, and are given only for victories. Bonus points are awarded for the extra kudos in winning races on foreign soil.

Each rider is awarded points for each win throughout his career. This is harmful to those for whom only a handful of the present top 20 were available, but then it was clearly easier for them to win every major race in a season that contained only three or four such races than in a season that contains 20, some of them overlapping.

The second ranking includes only those riders with a score of 100 or better on the first. It calculates the proportion of points they won during their professional careers relative to all the points theoretically available. This method ignores the fact that some races overlap and that it is therefore impossible for a contemporary rider to compete in them all, let alone win them all. This is harmful to the more modern riders—even Merckx never won more than seven of the top 20 races in a single season.

Each rider thus has two scores—a raw points total and a percentage amount of points gained in proportion to points available. Merckx tops both lists by a handsome margin. Converting both his scores to 1,000 allows for an arithmetic average. Other riders' raw scores are divided by 1,265 (Merckx's score) and multiplied by 1,000 to place them on the same scale as Merckx. To compare the percentage amount, Merckx's score is multiplied by 41.10152 to convert it to 1,000. Multiplying others' scores by the same amount places them on the same scale as Merckx for percentage points. Finally an overall score is figured by adding the two scores for each rider and dividing the result by two. Merckx remains at 1,000 and all other riders are ranked in relation to him.

I don't claim that this method is statistically valid, but it does seem to be a reasonable way of considering both the value of a high total of raw points and the value of a high proportion of percentage points for every rider. No adjustments have been made for those with unusually long or short careers.

The results will not please everybody, perhaps not anybody—we all have our favorites. Mine happens to be Bobet, who is 10th on raw points alone, but is out of the top 20 on percentage. Overall he is 14th, which may seem low, but the truth is that while Bobet specialized in winning very impressively, he didn't win that often.

TABLE 1

POINTS ALLOCATED TO TOP 20 RACES

Points awarded for win:

50	Tour de France	15	Bordeaux-Paris
40	World Championship		Grand Prix of Nations
30	Paris-Roubaix		Paris-Brussels
	Tour of Italy	10	Amstel Gold Race
25	Liège-Bastogne-Liège		Ghent-Wevelgem
	Tour of Flanders		Henninger Tower Grand Prix
	Tour of Lombardy		Het Volk
20	Flèche Wallonne		Tour of Switzerland
	Milan-San Remo		Zürich Championship
	Paris-Tours		
	Tour of Spain		

Bonus points awarded for win by a foreigner:
10	Tour de France
	Tour of Italy
5	All others, except none for world championship

Points for races held in wartime:
One-half the usual points for races held in 1915–1918 and 1940–1944, rounded down (e.g. 25 becomes 12). For the 1941–1942 Grand Prix of Nations, 4 points are awarded, since there were two versions of this race each year, one in the occupied zone and one in the free zone.

TABLE 2

HENDERSON'S COMPARATIVE RANKING OF THE TOP 70 RIDERS

Rider	(a)	(b)	(c)	(d)	(e)	(f)	(g)
1. Merckx	65–78/14	1365	1000	5610	24.33	1000	1000
2. Hinault	75–86/12	765	560.7	4910	15.58	640.4	600.6
3. Lapize	09–14/6	220	161.2	1315	16.73	687.6	424.4
4. Coppi	40–59/20	580	425.1	5868	9.88	406.1	415.6
5. Anquetil	53–69/17	550	403.1	6640	8.28	340.3	371.7
6. Binda	22–36/15	410	300.5	4425	9.27	381.0	340.8
7. Faber	06–14/9	215	157.5	1805	11.91	489.5	323.5
8. van Looy	53–70/18	485	355.5	7035	6.89	283.2	319.4
9. Bartali	35–54/20	402	294.7	5638	7.13	293.1	293.9
10. Gimondi	65–78/14	400	293.2	5610	7.13	293.1	293.2
11. de Vlaeminck	69–83/15	410	300.5	6060	6.77	278.3	289.4
12. Raas	75–83/9	290	212.5	3690	7.86	323.1	267.8
13. Pélissier	11–28/18	280	205.2	3643	7.69	316.1	260.7
14. Bobet	47–61/15	335	245.5	5725	5.85	240.4	243.0
15. Kelly	77–88/12	285	208.8	4910	5.80	240.1	224.5
16. Moser	73–88/16	325	238.2	6550	4.96	203.5	221.1
17. Maertens	72–81/10	250	183.2	4070	6.14	252.4	217.8
18. Petit-Breton	02–14/13	165	120.9	2160	7.64	314.0	217.5
19. Garrigou	07–14/8	125	91.6	1565	7.99	328.4	210.0
20. Thijs	12–27/16	202	148.1	3158	6.40	263.0	205.6
21. Bottecchia	22–27/6	120	87.9	1555	7.72	317.3	202.6
22. Kubler	40–57/18	260	190.5	5088	5.11	210.0	200.3
23. van Steenbergen	43–66/24	307	225.0	8427	3.64	149.6	187.3
24. Garin	93–11/19	125	91.6	1820	6.87	282.4	187.0
25. Brunero	20–29/10	160	117.2	2645	6.01	247.0	182.1
26. van Springel	65–81/17	270	197.9	6840	3.95	162.4	180.2
27. de Bruyne	53–61/9	185	135.6	3445	5.37	220.7	178.2
28. Girardengo	12–36/25	245	179.5	6028	4.06	166.8	173.2
29. Ronsse	26–38/13	190	139.2	4090	4.65	191.1	165.2
30. Janssen	62–72/11	195	142.9	4350	4.48	184.1	163.5
31. Fignon	82–88/7	150	109.9	2860	5.24	215.4	162.7
32. van Hauwaert	07–14/8	100	73.3	1665	6.01	247.0	160.2
33. Frantz	23–34/12	165	120.9	3440	4.80	197.3	159.1
34. Saronni	77–88/12	200	146.6	4910	4.07	167.3	157.0
35. Schotte	40–59/20	217	159.1	5868	3.70	152.1	155.6
36. Magne	26–39/14	185	135.6	4385	4.22	173.4	154.5
37. Argentin	81–88/8	155	113.6	3270	4.74	194.8	154.2
38. de Roo	58–68/11	175	128.2	4350	4.02	165.2	146.7
39. Magni	41–56/16	180	131.9	4643	3.88	159.5	145.7
40. Godefroot	65–79/15	205	150.2	6020	3.41	140.2	145.2
41. Roche	81–88/8	140	102.6	3270	4.28	175.9	139.3
42. Simpson	59–67/9	145	106.3	3565	4.07	167.3	136.8
43. Koblet	46–58/13	170	124.6	4905	3.47	142.6	133.6

TABLE 2 (CONTINUED)

HENDERSON'S COMPARATIVE RANKING OF THE TOP 70 RIDERS

44. Zoetemelk	70–88/19	210	153.9	7705	2.73	112.2	133.1
45. Suter	18–41/24	195	142.9	6490	3.00	123.3	133.1
46. Gyssels	30–36/7	105	76.9	2310	4.55	187.0	132.0
47. Leducq	27–39/13	150	109.9	4145	3.62	148.8	129.4
48. Maes	32–48/17	155	113.6	4388	3.53	145.1	129.3
49. Mottiat	12–25/14	110	80.6	2638	4.17	171.4	126.0
50. Lambot	08–24/17	120	87.9	3188	3.76	154.5	121.2
51. Speicher	32–45/14	120	87.9	3268	3.67	150.8	119.4
52. van der Poel	81–88/8	120	87.9	3270	3.67	150.8	119.4
53. Kuiper	73–88/16	175	128.2	6550	2.67	109.7	119.0
54. Deman	11–25/15	105	76.9	2843	3.69	151.7	114.3
55. Gaul	53–65/13	140	102.6	5045	2.78	114.3	108.5
56. Rebry	26–40/15	130	95.3	4440	2.93	120.4	107.5
57. Guerra	29–42/14	115	84.3	3806	3.02	124.1	104.2
58. Altig	60–71/12	130	95.3	4740	2.74	112.6	104.0
59. Belloni	15–31/17	109	79.9	3628	3.00	123.3	101.6
60. Derycke	50–62/13	130	95.3	4975	2.61	107.3	101.3
61. LeMond	81–88/8	100	73.3	3270	3.06	125.8	99.6
62. Kint	35–51/17	120	87.9	4538	2.64	108.5	98.2
63. Reybroeck	64–73/10	105	76.9	3960	2.65	108.9	92.9
64. Anderson	80–88/9	100	73.3	3680	2.72	111.8	92.6
65. Ockers	41–56/16	105	76.9	4643	2.26	92.9	84.9
66. Ocana	67–77/11	100	73.3	4390	2.28	93.7	83.5
67. Peeters	74–88/15	115	84.3	6140	1.87	76.9	80.6
68. Stablinski	53–68/16	115	84.3	6245	1.84	75.6	80.0
69. Thévenet	70–81/12	100	73.3	4845	2.06	84.7	79.0
70. Impanis	47–63/17	100	73.3	6525	1.53	62.9	68.1

COLUMN KEY

(a) The period of a rider's professional career and number of years as professional (e.g., Merckx 1965–78, 14 years).

(b) The total points gained through victory in qualifying races.

(c) Conversion of points in column (b) to 1,000 for Merckx and proportionally for all others.

(d) The maximum points available during each rider's professional career.

(e) The percentage of points actually scored from those available.

(f) Conversion of percentage in column (e) to 1,000 for Merckx and proportionally for all other riders.

(g) The final score for each rider—the arithmetic average of columns (c) and (f).

TABLE 3

HENDERSON'S RANKING OF TOP 20 RIDERS

Based On Aggregate Points		Based On Percentage Points	
1. Merckx	1365	1. Merckx	24.33
2. Hinault	765	2. Lapize	16.73
3. Coppi	580	3. Hinault	15.58
4. Anquetil	550	4. Faber	11.91
5. van Looy	485	5. Coppi	9.88
6. Binda	410	6. Binda	9.27
de Vlaeminck	410	7. Anquetil	8.28
8. Bartali	402	8. Garrigou	7.99
9. Gimondi	400	9. Raas	7.86
10. Bobet	335	10. Bottecchia	7.72
11. Moser	325	11. Pélissier, H.	7.69
12. van Steenbergen	307	12. Petit-Breton	7.64
13. Raas	290	13. Bartali	7.13
14. Kelly	285	14. Gimondi	7.13
15. Pélissier, H.	280	15. van Looy	6.89
16. van Springel	270	16. Garin	6.87
17. Kubler	260	17. de Vlaeminck	6.77
18. Maertens	250	18. Thijs	6.40
19. Girardengo	245	19. Maertens	6.14
20. Lapize	220	20. Brunero	6.01

Aggregate points are a rider's pro career total according to the allocations in Table 1.

Percentage points are the ratio of a rider's aggregate points to the total theoretically available to be won during his pro career.

TABLE 4

ALPHABETICAL LIST OF RIDERS WHO HAVE WON AT LEAST ONE OF THE 20 RACES

Adorni	85	Anthonis	10	†Bartali	402
Aerenhouts	20	Archambaud	15	Barthélémy	20
Aerts	55	†Argentin	155	Basso	40
Agostoni	20	Arras	15	Battaglin	55
Aimar, Louis	19	Aucouturier	90	Beaugendre	20
Aimar, Lucien	50	Augereau	15	Beccia	40
†Altig	130	Bahamontes	60	Beckaert	40
Amberg	10	Bal	30	Beheyt	50
Andersen	25	Baldini	90	Bellonne	15
†Anderson	100	Balmanion	75	†Belloni	109
†Anquetil	550	Baronchelli	65	Benoît	20

TABLE 4 (CONTINUED)

ALPHABETICAL LIST OF RIDERS WHO HAVE WON AT LEAST ONE OF THE 20 RACES

Bergamaschi	30	Caritoux	25	del Cancia	20
Berrendero	20	Carrara	8	Délépine	15
Berthon	15	Cerami	70	Delgado	80
Bertoglio	30	Chalmel	15	Deloor, A.	25
Beugels	15	Champion	30	Deloor, G.	50
Bevilacqua	35	Chesi	20	†Deman	105
†Binda	410	Chocque	15	de Meersman	20
Bini	37	Christophe	75	de Meyer	50
Bitossi	95	Cieleska	15	de Middeleir	10
Blattmann	20	Cinelli	35	de Mol	35
Blomme	20	Claes	70	Demulder	25
†Bobet	335	Clerici	50	de Muynck	40
Bocklandt	25	Cogan	15	Demuysère	25
Bodart	20	Conterno	40	den Hartog	35
Bogaerts	20	Contini	30	de Pauw	20
Bonduel	80	†Coppi, F.	580	Depoorter	37
Bontempi	50	Coppi, S.	35	Depredomme	50
Bordini	25	Corlaito	10	Dernies	15
†Bottecchia	120	Cornet	80	†de Roo	175
Boucquet	20	Coste	15	Dervaes	25
Bouhours	30	Cottereau	15	†Derycke	130
Bouvet	20	Criquielion	85	de Simpelaere	25
Bovet	20	Crupelandt	80	Desmet, A.	15
Bracke	45	Cuniolo	25	Desmet, G.	45
Braeckeveldt	20	Daems	90	†de Vlaeminck	410
Brambilla	25	Dancelli	45	de Vos	50
Braun	10	Danguillaume	30	de Waele	65
Breu	10	Danneels	75	de Witte	25
Brocco	20	Darrigade	70	de Wolf, A.	75
Brun	10	da Silva	15	de Wolf, H.	20
†Brunero	160	de Baere	10	D'Hooghe	25
Bruyère	80	Debaets	65	Dierickx	55
Buchwalder	10	†de Bruyne	185	Diggelmann	5
Bulla	30	de Cabooter	55	Diot	20
Buse	30	de Caluwé	60	Dolman	30
Buysse, A.	36	de Clerck	20	Dotto	25
Buysse, L.	60	de Cock	25	Duclos-Lasalle	15
Buysse, M.	25	Defilippis	25	Duerloo	25
Cadolle	15	Defraye	85	Dupont	40
Cainero	15	de Haan	25	Egg	25
Calzolari	30	de Hertoq	25	Egli	25
Camellini	25	de Jonghe	35	Elliott, S.	15
Camusso	30	Delathouwer	20	Engels	25
Caput	20	Delbecque	60	Enrici	50

TABLE 4 (CONTINUED)

ALPHABETICAL LIST OF RIDERS WHO HAVE WON AT LEAST
ONE OF THE 20 RACES

Erne	10	Grysolle	45	Landi	25
Ernzer	30	Guegan	20	Langarica	20
Everaert	20	Gueguen	20	Lapébie	50
†Faber	215	†Guerra	115	†Lapize	220
Faignaert	25	Guyot	10	Laurent, Marc	30
Favalli	10	†Gyssels	105	Laurent, Mic.	25
Fezzardi	15	Hagmann	10	Lauritzen	15
†Fignon	150	Hampsten	70	Leclercq	25
Fischer, Jean	20	Hanegraaf	30	†Leducq	150
Fischer, Jos.	55	Hardiquest	25	le Grèves	20
Fondriest	40	Hendrickx	30	Lejarreta	20
Foré	70	Herckenrath	25	Leman	75
Forestier	60	Herrera	25	†LeMond	100
Fornara	60	Heusghem	25	Leoni	10
Fossati	25	†Hinault	765	Lesna	90
†Frantz	165	Hoban	30	le Strat	15
Fuchs	30	Hoevenaers	20	Linard	15
Fuente	55	Hoste	10	Linari	20
Gabica	20	Houa	25	Linton	20
Galetti	60	Houyoux	25	Litzschi	20
Ganna	50	Huret	15	Lorono	20
Gardier	25	Huschke	15	Louviot	20
†Garin	125	Huysmans	20	Lubberding	15
Garnier	15	Idée	4	Madiot	30
†Garrigou	125	†Impanis	100	Maechler	25
Gaudin	10	Jacobs	15	†Maertens	250
†Gaul	140	†Janssen	195	Maes, R.	60
Gauthier	60	Janssens	20	†Maes, S.	155
Gavazzi	40	Junkermann	55	Maffeo	15
Geldermans	30	Kaers	65	†Magne	185
Georget	30	Kamber	10	†Magni	180
Gerbi	25	Karstens	25	Mahe	50
Geyer	15	Kaspar	10	Mantelet	10
†Gimondi	400	†Kelly	285	Mara	45
†Girardengo	245	Keteleer	20	Marchisio	30
Gisiger	40	Kherkove	10	Maréchal	20
Glaus	20	†Kindt	120	Martens	45
Goasmat	4	Knecht	40	Martin, Hans	10
†Godefroot	205	Knetemann	75	Martin, Hector	20
Gölz	60	†Koblet	170	Martinet	5
Gomez	25	†Kubler	260	Masson, E., Sr.	20
Graf	25	†Kuiper	175	Masson, E., Jr.	75
Gremo	20	†Lambot	120	Mattioda	15
Groussard	25	Lammerts	30	Maule	25

TABLE 4 (CONTINUED)

ALPHABETICAL LIST OF RIDERS WHO HAVE WON AT LEAST
ONE OF THE 20 RACES

Maurer	20	Peeters, W.	10	Roman	15
Maye	70	Pélissier, F.	50	Ronchini	25
Melckenbeeck	55	†Pélissier, H.	280	†Ronsse	190
†Merckx	1365	Pesarradona	20	Rooks	55
Mertens	25	Pesenti	30	Rosiers	35
Merviel	20	†Petit-Breton	165	Rosseel	10
Meulenberg	80	Petrucci	60	Rossi	64
Meunier	35	Petterson	40	Ruegg	20
Meyer	20	Pfenniger	20	Ruiz	20
Michelotto	25	Piemontese	25	Ruperez	20
Michiels	15	Pieters, A.	10	†Saronni	200
Middelkamp	40	Pieters, P.	25	Schaer	20
Mills	20	Pingeon	75	Schellenberg	10
Minardi	25	Pino	20	Schepers	75
Mithouard	15	Pintens	95	Schils	25
Moineau	20	Planckaert, E.	45	†Schotte	217
Mollin	25	Planckaert, J.	35	Schoubben	40
Mollo	25	Planckaert, W.	40	Schuiten	55
Monséré	70	Poblet	50	Scieur	85
Moresi	10	Poels	15	Scodeller	25
Moser, A.	20	Poggiali	40	Sellier	80
†Moser, F.	325	Pollentier	80	Sels	40
Motta	70	Portaluppi	15	Sercu	10
Mottard	15	Post	35	Sieger	5
Mottet	75	Pottier	50	†Simpson	145
†Mottiat	110	Poulidor	90	Soldani	25
Moujica	15	Preziosi	30	Soler	20
Müller	40	Prim	20	Somers	47
Naef	5	Privat	25	†Speicher	120
Nédélec	15	†Raas	290	†Stablinski	115
Negrini	25	Ramon	25	Steevens	10
Nencini	90	Rault	20	Stéphane	15
Nijdam	10	Reboul	20	Sterckx	75
Noret	15	†Rebry	130	Storme	35
Notter	10	†Reybrouck	105	Suarez	20
†Ocana	100	Rheinwald	10	†Suter	195
†Ockers	105	Ricci	37	Swerts	45
Ollivier	10	Rinaldi	15	Taccone	25
Olmo	40	Ritserveldt	25	Tamames	20
Oriani	55	Rivierre	45	Tassin	15
Ottenbros	40	Robic	50	Taverne	15
Pambianco	50	†Roche	140	Teisseire	10
Passérieu	50	Rodriguez, D.	40	†Thévenet	100
†Peeters, L.	115	Rodriguez, E.	20	Thiberghiem	25

TABLE 4 (CONTINUED)

ALPHABETICAL LIST OF RIDERS WHO HAVE WON AT LEAST ONE OF THE 20 RACES

Thurau	45	†van Hauwaert	100	Vermandel	75
Thijs, K.	10	van Holen	10	Verschoore	25
†Thijs, P.	202	van Impe	60	Verschueren	90
Tinazzi	15	van Leerberghe	25	Verwaecke	50
Torricelli	12	van Linden	50	Visentini	30
Trousselier	95	†van Looy	485	Wagner	5
Tschan	25	van Meenen	10	Walkowiak	50
Valetti	75	van Neste	15	Wampers	15
Vallet	15	Vannitsen	20	Wattelier	15
van Coningsloo	35	van Ryckeghem	15	Wechselberger	15
van Daele	60	van Rysselberghe	20	Weilemann	20
van den Broucke	45	†van Springel	270	Wellens	15
van den Haute	10	†van Steenbergen	307	Wesemael	15
Vanderaerden	85	van Sweevelt	25	Willems	60
†van der Poel	120	van Tyghem	25	Wolfshohl	25
van der Velde	15	Vekemans	20	Wouters	40
van Dyck	25	Verbeeck	55	Zandegu	30
van Eename	10	van Vliet, L.	15	Zilioli	15
van Est	90	van Vliet, T.	25	Zimmermann, R.	15
van Genechten	20	Verhaegen	15	Zimmermann, U.	10
van Hevel	60	Verlinden	15	†Zoetemelk	210

† Riders with 100 points are among the top 70 to date and are also ranked in Table 2.

Appendix 2

Bibliography

A.

Three books are indispensable for the comprehensive information they contain:

P. Chany	La Fabuleuse Histoire du Cyclisme, Volume 1 1975; Volume 2 1979	O.D.I.L., Paris
R. Jacobs, H. Mahau, H. Van den Bremt and R. Pirotte	Vélo Gotha	Presses de Belgique, Brussels 1984

B.

Four books to which I have made specific reference:

J. Anquetil	Anquetil	Hatier, Paris 1971
M. Girardet, J. Régali, A. Burtin, J-P. Estoppey and J-P. Mérot	Les Heures Glorieuses du Cyclisme Suisse	Edita, Lausanne 1981
N. G. Henderson	Contintental Cycling Racing	Pelham, London 1970
T. Simpson	Cycling is my Life	Stanley Paul, London 1966

C.

Other recommended works:

J. Augendre	Histoires du Cyclisme	Calmann-Lévy, Paris 1966
R. Bastide	Le Légende des Pélissier	Presses de la Cité, Paris 1981
G. Briquet	60 Ans du Tour de France	Table Ronde, Paris 1962
J. Bobet	Louison Bobet	Gallimard, Paris 1958
P. Chany	Arriva Coppi	Table Ronde, Paris 1960
J-M. Leblanc	Les Pavés du Nord	Table Ronde, Paris 1982
T. Mathy	Les Géants du Cyclisme Belge	Arts et Voyages, Brussels 1974
F. Terbéen	Les Géants du Cyclisme	Del Duca, Paris 1969

D.

Regular sources:

Cycling Weekly	Published in Surrey, England
L'Equipe	Published daily except Sundays, Paris
Vélo	Published annually in Brussels
International Cycle Sport	No longer published, but from 1970–1984 published a series of paperback booklets about cycling: worth sending for a list of what's available to: Mr. D. Fretwell, Kennedy & Cox Ltd., Healey Works, Goulbourne Street, Keighley, West Yorkshire, England.
VeloNews	Published in Boulder, Colorado
Winning	Published in Allentown, Pennsylvania

Index

Pages in italic indicate that a photo of that subject appears on the cited page. Races are cited only outside their chapters.